THE Instant Pot
DIABETES COOKBOOK

SIMPLE RECIPES FOR HEALTHY HOME COOKING

NANCY S. HUGHES

American
Diabetes
Association.

Associate Publisher, Books, Abe Ogden; *Director, Book Operations,* Victor Van Beuren; *Managing Editor, Books,* John Clark; *Associate Director, Book Marketing,* Annette Reape; *Acquisitions Editor,* Jaclyn Konich; *Senior Manager, Book Editing,* Lauren Wilson; *Composition,* Circle Graphics; *Cover Design,* Vis-à-vis Creative; *Photographer,* Renee Comet Photography; *Printer,* Imago.

Printed in Republic of Poland

1 3 5 7 9 10 8 6 4 2

The suggestions and information contained in this publication are generally consistent with the *Standards of Medical Care in Diabetes* and other policies of the American Diabetes Association, but they do not represent the policy or position of the Association or any of its boards or committees. Reasonable steps have been taken to ensure the accuracy of the information presented. However, the American Diabetes Association cannot ensure the safety or efficacy of any product or service described in this publication. Individuals are advised to consult a physician or other appropriate health care professional before undertaking any diet or exercise program or taking any medication referred to in this publication. Professionals must use and apply their own professional judgment, experience, and training and should not rely solely on the information contained in this publication before prescribing any diet, exercise, or medication. The American Diabetes Association—its officers, directors, employees, volunteers, and members—assumes no responsibility or liability for personal or other injury, loss, or damage that may result from the suggestions or information in this publication.

Madelyn L. Wheeler conducted the internal review of this book to ensure that it meets American Diabetes Association guidelines.

☺The paper in this publication meets the requirements of the ANSI Standard Z39.48-1992 (permanence of paper).

ADA titles may be purchased for business or promotional use or for special sales. To purchase more than 50 copies of this book at a discount, or for custom editions of this book with your logo, contact the American Diabetes Association at the address below or at booksales@diabetes.org.

American Diabetes Association
2451 Crystal Drive, Suite 900
Arlington, VA 22202

DOI: 10.2337/9781580407069

Library of Congress Cataloging-in-Publication Data

Names: Hughes, Nancy S, author.
Title: The Instant Pot diabetes cookbook : simple recipes for healthy home cooking / Nancy S. Hughes.
Description: Arlington, VA : American Diabetes Association, 2019. | Includes index. | Summary: "This Instant Pot-authorized cookbook from the experts at the American Diabetes Association contains 90 easy, diabetes-friendly recipes made with simple ingredients that will easily transform into mouth-watering meals. New to using an Instant Pot? No problem! Each recipe includes detailed instructions to make cooking with your Instant Pot a breeze. Whatever you're craving, you'll find it in this book-from family favorites to a wide range of recipes inspired by Mexican, Italian, Thai, Indian, and Cajun cuisines. Additionally, each recipe meets the nutrition guidelines set by the American Diabetes Association for diabetes and heart-healthy eating"-- Provided by publisher.
Identifiers: LCCN 2019033773 (print) | LCCN 2019033774 (ebook) | ISBN 9781580407069 (paperback) | ISBN 9781580407212 (ebook)
Subjects: LCSH: Diabetes--Diet therapy. | Smart cookers. | LCGFT: Cookbooks.
Classification: LCC RC662 .H838 2019 (print) | LCC RC662 (ebook) | DDC 641.5/6314--dc23
LC record available at https://lccn.loc.gov/2019033773
LC ebook record available at https://lccn.loc.gov/2019033774

Dedication

To my husband, Greg! Even though I had lots of other help, you were always willing to run by the store for one more item, listen to one more idea, taste one more recipe, or wash a pressure cooker pot insert (or two, or three, or four) so I could start on another recipe again and again and again!

Don't think I didn't notice . . . again and again and again!

Thank you!

and

To my big kids and my little kids: Will, Kelly, Molly, Anna Flynn, Hootie, Annie, Terry, Jilli, Jesse, Emma, Lucy, Taft, Kara, River, and Merritt. Fifteen reasons to pull out that pressure cooker and leave it out!

Acknowledgments

To Abe Ogden, Victor Van Beuren, Jaclyn Konich, and Lauren Wilson, my "people" at the American Diabetes Association: Thanks for being behind my efforts, believing in me, and getting excited with me! I know I get carried away—that's only because I care about the American Diabetes Association and what I can "bring to the table"!

To Sylvia Vollmer, my kitchen assistant: You're right there every single time I call! You lead a "juggling act" life because of me, and I thank you ever so much!

To Melanie McKibbin, my office manager: Your "to do" list is never-ending. If you turn the list over, there's more on the back! And you "fix it" . . . you always do!

Contents

2 Protein, Veggie, and Grain Main Dish Salads 41

3 Sandwiches: Open-Faced, Wrapped, Stuffed, and Between the Bun 55

4 Soups, Stews, and Anything in a Bowl 69

7   So Simple Protein-Based Entrées   121

8 Sides: Starchy and Nonstarchy 137

9 Sweet Enders 155

BUSY? WHO'S NOT?

Then why not get some help and simplify your life—especially in the kitchen! Electric pressure cookers, like the Instant Pot, are a great kitchen tool that most people either have in their kitchens or have heard a lot about.

So, what is the big deal with Instant Pots, anyway? Well, when you use an Instant Pot, you don't have to preheat the oven, light up the grill, make a mess on your stove top, or wash a lot of pots and pans . . . none of that! You cook *everything* in one pot! The best part is that it cuts the cooking time *way down*. Just plug in your Instant Pot and let it do the work! It's really that simple! It's about 50–70% faster than other cooking methods, so it saves time and energy (both the electric bill type energy and your own energy, too!).

Cooking with an Instant Pot may help *retain* some nutrients in foods, such as water soluble vitamins (which can be lost when a food is cooked in water). It also *retains* the natural flavors of the foods.

This appliance is clean, quiet, consistent, and it takes up about the same amount of space on your counter or in your cupboard as a slow cooker. Now *that's* what's so great about an Instant Pot!

Why not take advantage of a good thing when it can help you take care of yourself and those you care about the most?

WHY THIS BOOK?

Because of the wildly popular demand for the Instant Pot, there are quite a number of electric pressure cooker cookbooks on the market right now, including some that are marketed as healthy. But keep in mind that just because a recipe is called "healthy" does not mean that it is right for people with diabetes. Healthy recipes in general are good, but they do vary in their ingredients and nutritional information and are not necessarily appropriate for people with diabetes . . . *these recipes are*!

Every single recipe in this book meets the nutrition guidelines of the trusted health organization the American Diabetes Association. That means that every recipe stays within the criteria the American Diabetes Association has set for calories, carbohydrates, saturated fat, sodium, sugar, and other nutrients. These recipes were purposefully written for people with diabetes, as well as for those who want to help prevent diabetes while simply enjoying tasty, nutritious meals.

I'm sure some of you are familiar with my cookbooks already. I've written 12 cookbooks now for the American Diabetes Association. That's well over 1,000 diabetes-friendly recipes just for the American Diabetes Association alone. I like to keep things simple. All the ingredients in this book are "normal" ingredients that you can find in your supermarket. My recipes are easy to follow, easy on the budget, loaded with flavor, and geared toward people who are "on the go" no matter what stage of life they're in. In other words, my recipes are doable and delicious!

When it came to learning to cook with an Instant Pot, I was overwhelmed at first, just like most of us are with new appliances. I mean, I really, really was! So I kept that feeling in mind when writing this book. I wanted to keep the ingredients and the directions *very* simple.

I've narrowed down the basic information about the Instant Pot in this introduction so it doesn't feel like a "cut and pasted" manual. In fact, this is not to be used in place of the manual for your Instant Pot. There's a lot of noteworthy information in that little manual that you should use for reference. Didn't hold on to your manual? Then just go online to the Instant Pot website (www.instantpot.com)!

Again, I'm trying to keep things as *simple* and *straightforward* as possible.

There are 90 recipes in this book, including family favorites, such as the shredded meats and hearty chilis, of course, and a wide range of flavors from Mexican, Italian, American, Thai, Indian, and Cajun cuisines. Every part of the day is included: breakfast, lunch, dinner, appetizers, sides, and desserts.

Most of the recipes in this book are designed to serve 4 people. I felt it was important to keep the number of servings low, as making more servings than needed could lead to overeating or eating too many carbs! Those recipes can be doubled if you need to feed more than 4 people. There *are* some recipes in my book that make 8 servings, but only those that can be frozen successfully or can be served again later in the week.

Each recipe will include the "Hands-On" time (which means you're involved), "Hands-Off" time (which means you're *not* involved!), and "Total" time (which means from start to finish). The recipes will also include the total yield, number of servings, and serving size.

HOW DOES THE INSTANT POT WORK?

I used a 6-quart electric pressure cooker (the Instant Pot Lux60 V3 6-Quart 6-in-1 Multi-Use Programmable version) for all of the recipes in this book, and I believe that's a standard model on the market today.

An Instant Pot does the work of multiple appliances—it's a slow cooker, steamer, rice cooker, sauté pan, warming pot, and pressure cooker all in one. That's all great, but in this book I am only using the Instant Pot as a pressure cooker in Pressure Cook mode to keep things simple for beginners and for myself.

I don't like to plan too far ahead or spend a lot of time figuring out which buttons to push when. So when I was developing these recipes, I used the two most widely used buttons on the Instant Pot: the Manual or Pressure Cook button and the Sauté button. (The Sauté button may be labeled "Browning" on some brands and models of pressure cookers.) The Manual/Pressure Cook button is used "under pressure," and the Sauté button is used to brown food in the beginning of the cooking process or to reduce liquid at the end.

When using the Manual/Pressure Cook function, some Instant Pot models allow you to select high or low pressure, but not all models give you this option. My model, for example, does not allow me to select between high and low pressure. Check the manual for your model to see if your model allows you to select a pressure. I have not specified high or low pressure in the recipe instructions when using the Manual/Pressure Cook function, but if your Instant Pot model allows you to select a pressure, choose high pressure for these recipes.

When using the Sauté function, you can adjust the temperature just as you would if you were sautéing something on the stove. Simply press the Sauté button, then press the Adjust button until you reach the desired temperature. These recipes call for you to adjust the temperature to "More" or "High" when sautéing.

It's simple: you can start with the Manual/Pressure Cook function, or you can switch it from Manual/Pressure Cook to Sauté (or vice versa) as needed. That's it. *That is it!*

TIMING

The most common issue I hear people bring up about pressure cookers is that they take time to come to pressure. But look at it this way: if you were trying to bring something to a boil on top of the stove in a regular pot, that would take time too. The speed of an Instant Pot really comes from the pressurized cooking time—it slashes the actual cooking time completely in half! Now *that's* where the time saver actually is. Plus the Instant Pot seals in the nutritional benefits of the foods you're cooking rather than letting them boil away!

When using an Instant Pot, timing (both for the preparation of the food and the actual cooking of the food) is not an exact science. Use the times I've provided in this book as a general guide rather than a strict set of parameters. There are many variables that can affect timing, including the size and weight of ingredients, seasonings, temperature of the food, and altitude, so consider my recommendations as a general starting point.

If you removed the lid and see that the dish isn't completely done, the best thing to do is press the Cancel button, always checking to make sure the silicone ring insert is secured in place, then seal the lid, and set the Manual/Pressure Cook button for 2–3 minutes. I've found that it is much easier to lock the lid (align it) after the Cancel button is pressed.

Each recipe in this book includes:

HANDS-ON TIME: This includes all preparation of the ingredients and anything else you do before the Instant Pot is sealed. I tried to pace things as a home cook would, but some people are faster or slower than others with chopping, rinsing, and measuring. Work at the pace that is comfortable for you.

HANDS-OFF TIME: This includes the time it takes for the Instant Pot to build up pressure before the actual cooking time begins plus the cooking time and any natural pressure release time. Note: The Manual/Pressure Cook time is the actual cooking time where the food is under pressure.

TOTAL TIME: This includes the entire time it takes to complete the recipe, from the time you start to the time it is finished.

I've included a "basic" cooking times chart derived from my findings working with an Instant Pot. This covers many of the ingredients used in this book. These are very basic, general guidelines only, to help get you started and give you an idea of how much time to allow when cooking an ingredient by itself. For more information, refer to your Instant Pot manual or their website.

Below are the ingredients most commonly used in this book:

Seafood	Cooking Time (Minutes)	
	Fresh	Frozen
Fish, fillet (1/2 inch thick)	2	3
Fish, fillet (3/4–1 inch thick)	3	4
Shrimp or prawn	1–2	2–4

Rice & Grains	Ratio (Grain:Water)	Cooking Time (Minutes)
Farro	1:2	7
Oats, steel cut	1:3	3
Quinoa, organic/natural (not quick cooking)	1:2	2
Rice, brown	3/4:1	20
Rice, wild	1:2	20
Wheat berries	1:3	25

Dried Legumes (Unsoaked)	Ratio (Legume:Water)	Cooking Time (Minutes)
Black beans	1:4	25
Chickpeas (garbanzo beans)	1:4	35
Lima beans, large	1:4	12
Navy beans	1:4	45
Pinto beans	1:4	40
Lentils, green/brown	1:4	7–8
Peas, split green	1:4	12

Poultry & Meat	Cooking Time (Minutes)
Poultry	
Chicken breast, boneless	5/5/5 (5 under pressure/ 5 natural pressure release/ 5 standing)
Chicken, whole	7 per lb
Chicken thigh, bone-in	10–15
Turkey breast, bone-in	6 per lb
Meat (Beef & Pork)	
Meatballs	5 per lb
Chuck, blade, brisket, round, shoulder (1–1 1/2-inch cubes)	15–20 per lb
Chuck, blade, brisket, shoulder (4-inch pieces) (fall apart)	30–40 per lb

Vegetables	Cooking Time (Minutes)	
	Fresh	Frozen
Artichoke (whole & trimmed)	15	
Artichoke, hearts		5–6
Asparagus (whole or cut)	1–2	
Beans, green	2–3	
Beetroot (small, whole)	11–13	
Beetroot (large, whole)	18	
Broccoli (florets)	0–1	
Brussels sprouts (whole)	2–3	
Cabbage, green (wedges)	7	
Carrots (sliced or shredded)	2–3	3–4
Carrots (whole or chunks)	6–8	
Cauliflower (florets)	2–3	
Celery (chunks)	2–3	
Corn (kernels)	1–2	2–3
Corn (on the cob)	3	
Eggplant (slices or chunks)	3–4	
Greens (chopped)	4–5	
Leeks	2–3	
Mixed vegetables	3–4	4–6
Okra	2–3	3–4
Onions (sliced)	2–3	3–4
Parsnips (chunks)	3–4	
Peas, green	1–2	1–2
Potatoes (cubed)	3–4	
Potatoes (small, whole)	8–10	
Potatoes (large, whole)	18	
Spinach	1–2	2–3
Squash, acorn (quarters)	5	

Vegetables	Cooking Time (Minutes)	
	Fresh	Frozen
Squash, spaghetti (halves)	7	
Sweet potato (cubes)	2–4	
Sweet potato (large, halves)	12–15	
Sweet potato (small, whole)	1–12	
Sweet pepper (slices or chunks)	1–3	2–4
Tomatoes (grape, whole)	5	

Fruits	Cooking Time (Minutes)	
	Fresh	Frozen
Apples (slices or pieces)	1–2	
Apples (whole)	3–4	
Berries		1
Peaches	2–3	4–5
Pears (whole, firm, not ripe)	2–3	
Pineapple (chunks)		4–5
Raisins		4–5

TECHNIQUE TIPS: WHAT TO DO WHEN A RECIPE SAYS . . .

DO NOT STIR: When browning an ingredient in an Instant Pot, it's very important not to turn or stir unless otherwise mentioned in the directions. By *not* moving an ingredient around, just keeping it in one place the whole time, you help the ingredient to brown better. If you stir it, even in small batches, it won't brown, but will "stew" instead. (This has a lot to do with the tall design of the pot, but using minimal amounts of oil and lean ingredients can affect the browning as well.) So, just leave the ingredients alone when browning.

LET STAND: There are two reasons to let a dish or ingredient stand before serving: 1) When a recipe calls for letting a protein stand a few minutes on a cutting board before slicing or shredding, that standing time allows the protein to continue cooking and reach the correct internal temperature. It also allows the protein to "relax" and the juices to redistribute; the texture will change during that time. Don't skip that step. 2) When a recipe calls for letting a dish that has finished cooking stand for 10 minutes or so before serving, it's usually to allow all of the flavors of the ingredients to take time to blend and/or to reach the desired texture.

WHEN SCREEN SAYS THE WORD "HOT": When you need to brown an ingredient before cooking under pressure, it is important not to add that ingredient until the screen says "HOT." The pot will not be hot enough before that point for the ingredient to brown properly.

RESET TO SAUTÉ AND BRING TO A BOIL: Pressure cooking retains the vast majority, if not all, of the liquid drawn from the ingredients as well as any liquid that may have been added initially to the pot. Little moisture, if any, escapes. Throughout this book, you'll see that I have you remove ingredients with a slotted spoon and reset to Sauté, bringing the remaining ingredients and any liquid to a boil for a certain amount of time. By using this method, it helps concentrate the really rich flavors and bring out the saltiness without overdoing it with added salt! It works every time!

FREEZES WELL: Some of these recipes will make enough servings so that a few portions can be frozen for later use. Always bring any portion that you intend to freeze to room temperature before placing in freezer. It's best to freeze portions in individual baggies or containers to help with portion control—that way you'll know you're getting the right serving size! Be sure to mark the package clearly and add the date while you're at it!

RINSE AND DRAIN: When cooking rice, beans, peas, or lentils, be sure to rinse them (and you may want to sort the beans, lentils, and peas, removing any random tiny stones as well) before adding them to the pressure cooker pot, unless the recipe specifically says not to. This helps the rice, beans, peas, or lentils cook more evenly and can make them less starchy in texture. Other ingredients, such as canned beans, need to be rinsed ahead of time to remove the "pasty" canning liquid. If you don't drain and rinse these canned products, the liquid can cloud the overall dish and mask the flavors of the other ingredients.

COAT WITH COOKING SPRAY: When coating ramekins or pans with nonstick cooking spray, place them in your kitchen sink and spray *there* rather than on your counter or while holding them in the air. This makes for easier cleanup since it's the sink that gets sprayed, not the counter or the floor!

CUT WINTER SQUASH: Get some help with the hard-to-cut stuff, like acorn and spaghetti squash. Make it easier on yourself by piercing the skin of the squash all over with the tip of a sharp knife. Microwave it on high setting for 1 1/2–2 minutes. This will soften the skin *slightly* and make it a bit easier to cut. It will still be firm but a bit more manageable.

INGREDIENT INFO: TIPS FOR WHAT TO BUY

The Frozen

FROZEN PEPPERS AND ONIONS: I use frozen peppers and onions quite often. It's a great way to save on prep and cleanup time—they're already cut and waiting for you! But you can always use the fresh variety, equal parts peppers and onions, if you prefer.

OTHER FROZEN VEGGIES: I use other frozen veggies quite often, too. Toss 'em in! No need to thaw, no need to chop, no need to mess up a cutting board or pull out a knife. Just measure them out and plop them in the pot! Again, you can use the fresh variety, but using frozen veggies cuts way down on the prep time, which, for me, is often the deciding factor on whether I make a recipe or not on some nights when I'm already exhausted.

STRAIGHT FROM THE FREEZER CHICKEN, MEAT, OR FISH: I'm sure you've heard that you can cook frozen chunks of meat and poultry in an Instant Pot. Well, you can, but it's best to use a flat, packaged item, such as a flat package of ground turkey or lean ground beef or chicken breasts that are frozen individually or at least in a single layer. Otherwise there's too much of a variance in how the item cooks. Big "hunks" or uneven thicknesses won't cook evenly.

The Pantry

MULTIGRAIN PASTA: You'll see that I often call for multigrain pasta. It has tons of fiber but is lighter in texture than the heavier whole-wheat varieties.

"HOT OR NOT" HOT SAUCE: Specific brands of hot sauce are suggested in my recipes. That is to let you know whether the variety is *hot* (such as Sriracha)—which is why a smaller amount is used—or *not as hot* (such as Frank's)—which is why a larger amount is used. (Note: These different hot sauce options contain different levels of salt that adds to the sodium value for the recipe, so the amounts used are the maximum allowed to meet the sodium guidelines of the American Diabetes Association.)

THE CUT OF THE ALMOND: I call for *slivered* almonds a lot, not the sliced kind, in this cookbook because the slivered variety give more texture and crunch and hold up while pressure cooking.

THE TURMERIC TRICK: Want to add a "snap" of bright yellow color to your regular brown rice dishes without the expense of saffron? Just add a bit of ground turmeric to the rice water before cooking!

The Fresh

POBLANO, POBLANO, POBLANO: I use poblano chile peppers instead of green bell peppers a lot! To me, poblanos give you so much more of a pepper flavor than the common bell pepper. But you can always substitute a small green bell pepper for every poblano chile pepper called for in these recipes, if you prefer. Poblano peppers do add a small amount of heat to a dish, but the amount varies from pepper to pepper.

FIRM AND RIPE: When a recipe calls for a firm or ripe fruit, pay attention. There's a reason for that. Sometimes the fruit needs to be firm to hold up and retain its shape and texture through the pressure-cooking process. Other times, it needs to be ripe in order to add to the sweetness of the dish or to break down during the pressure-cooking process and act as a natural thickening agent. It does matter!

FRESH CITRUS, THE REAL STUFF: For peak flavors, always use fresh lime or lemon juice instead of the concentrated, bottled variety.

POWER OF THE PEEL: Don't skip the zesting or grating of the peel from an orange or lemon—it adds a huge punch of flavor, heightens the freshness of the other ingredients, and brings out the citrus flavor without "watering down" the dish. Just don't use the white pith right beneath the peel. It's bitter.

GINGER DILEMMA: When a recipe calls for "grated fresh ginger," the best way to prepare the ginger is to cut off (or scrape away) the outer bark of the gingerroot and grate the pale yellow portion using a microplane grater or the fine side of a handheld grater. Grate across the grain of the fibers of the ginger. When buying ginger, figure that for every teaspoon of grated ginger needed you should buy a 1-inch length of gingerroot. Just break off the portion you need in the produce aisle—you don't need to buy a big hunk of ginger.

SAVING THE CILANTRO (AND PARSLEY): Storing cilantro and parsley used to feel like a waste of time to me. I tried everything and still ended up having to pitch them after a few days—until I started doing this! Treat fresh herbs like you would a bunch of fresh flowers! As soon as you get home from the grocery store, cut the ends of the stems off (about 1 inch from the bottom), stick the whole bunch in a wide-bottomed glass or jar of water, and store them in the fridge. They last a *whole lot* longer than they would just stored in your crisper. Using a wide-bottomed glass prevents it from tipping over easily.

MULTIGRAIN LOAF BREAD: You'll see that I call for multigrain Italian loaf bread frequently. It's a bit lighter in texture than the whole-wheat varieties and contains a good amount of fiber. You can find it in your grocer's bakery. Buy the whole loaf rather than the sliced variety.

BUY MORE MEAT? WHY? When buying cuts of beef or pork, always buy at least 8–12 oz more meat than the recipe calls for. There is usually at least 8–12 oz of fat on most cuts of chuck, brisket, or pork shoulder that should be removed and discarded before cooking. And because the amount of fat varies from cut to cut and store to store, the weight given in the ingredient list in the recipe is what the weight should be *after* it is trimmed of fat. So keep that in mind as you're shopping.

FISH THICKNESS: The thickness of a fish fillet does matter as far as cooking times are concerned. Pay attention to the thickness recommended in the ingredient list so you don't end up with dry or overcooked results. For example, a 1/2-inch-thick fish fillet should cook for only 2 minutes and a 3/4- to 1-inch-thick fish fillet should cook for only 3 minutes.

TOOLS TO HAVE ON HAND

METAL TRIVET: Most electric pressure cookers come with a trivet, but if yours didn't, a simple metal trivet will work. This is used to hold foods away from the liquid while cooking and prevent them from coming directly in contact with the bottom of the pot.

UTENSILS: Tongs or a long fork and spoon will aid in removing items at the end of the cooking time.

COLLAPSIBLE STEAMER BASKET: This comes in handy when trying to cook something that might be a little tricky to remove from the pressure cooker. Simply lift the whole basket up at once to remove the food.

6-OUNCE HEAT-PROOF RAMEKINS OR PYREX-STYLE CUSTARD CUPS: These ramekins/custard cups are used for individual breakfast egg dishes and desserts. They stack easily in the Instant Pot, too.

7-INCH NONSTICK SPRINGFORM PAN: A springform pan can be used for making various appetizers, desserts, and a variety of recipes that need to be covered with foil during the cooking process to avoid moisture. Springform pans are sold in the housewares section of major stores, but if they're not available at a store near you, you can definitely find them everywhere online!

FOOD SCALE: Just a little inexpensive variety is all you need, but you *do* need one in order to weigh out your ingredients. You want to make sure you have the right amount of each ingredient!

FOIL: Keep aluminum foil on hand to cover individual ramekins or an entire springform pan, and for making various "slings" to help lift items out of the pressure cooker pot easily and safely.

Nice to Have on Hand (Inexpensively!)

EXTRA TIMER: If you plan to leave the kitchen while the Instant Pot is cooking, set a timer that you can take out of the room with you or one that has a loud tone. The timer on the Instant Pot gives a gentle "ding" that goes off when the food is finished cooking. But it has a very light sound and you may not hear it if you're not close by. So you may want to set a timer that is louder or take a little timer with you. No need to purchase a kitchen timer; setting a timer on a mobile phone will work well.

RULER: A metal or plastic ruler is all you need, but it comes in handy when trying to measure ingredients, such as 1/2-inch cubes or 1-inch beef chunks. The size of the ingredients does matter for timing and successful end results.

EXTRA SILICONE RINGS: Buy an extra silicone ring or two for your Instant Pot lid to have on hand in case the lid gets too loose or starts having trouble staying in place, or the silicone ring has absorbed some of the stronger flavors from intense spices or from fish. Don't wait to order them or shop for them until you actually need them. Keep a couple on hand so you don't miss out on any meals. The easiest, most convenient way is to shop for them online or call around to see who carries rings for the model you need.

SILICONE SPATULAS: I really do recommend these—not that you have to have them, but I *love* them. I have countless inexpensive silicone spatulas. They're flexible, heatproof, and get every bit of food and sauce out of the pot, the bowl, or the jar!

LET'S GET STARTED!

So pull that Instant Pot out of the box it came in and plug it in!

I suggest you start out with some of my easiest of easy entrées:

- Freezer-Fix Chili (p. 74)
- Italian Parmesan Chicken Thighs (p. 127)
- Jalapeño–Avocado Salmon (p. 126)
- Green Bean and Feta Pasta Salad (p. 50)

There's a bit of a bonus when you start with these recipes. When you make the Freezer-Fix Chili or Italian Parmesan Chicken Thighs, any leftovers you may have are great to pop in the freezer for a grab-and-go lunch or dinner later on!

Do use your manual and the Instant Pot website from time to time for additional cooking charts, cleaning instructions, and troubleshooting information. I use both, especially the website. There's just so much information out there to absorb at one time, especially when you're just getting started. When you do flip through the manual or scroll down a webpage, you'll see that things make so much more sense and you'll have much more confidence now that your questions have been simplified for you!

Now, that's enough information to get you started.

So, here's how this will work:

> 2 buttons on your Instant Pot
> + simple directions
> + nutrition guidelines from the American Diabetes Association
> = a boatload of great-tasting, diabetes-friendly recipes!

That's it! Enjoy!

—Nancy Hughes

If you've just been diagnosed with diabetes or prediabetes, you're probably wondering what, when, and how much you need to eat. You may be surprised to hear that when it comes to diabetes nutrition there is no "one-size-fits-all" approach—no "diabetes diet" or perfect amount of nutrients (protein, fat, or even carbohydrates) that is right for every person with diabetes. Diabetes affects people of all ages, across all cultures, with all different health backgrounds, eating preferences, and budgets. So it makes sense that there is a variety of eating patterns that can help people manage diabetes. The eating pattern you follow should be personalized to meet your needs, fit your lifestyle, and help you achieve your health goals. With the help of your healthcare team, you can create an eating plan that will work best for you. A Registered Dietitian Nutritionist (RDN) or Certified Diabetes Educator (CDE) in particular can help you manage your diabetes or prediabetes through diet and lifestyle changes. Ask your primary care provider for a referral if an RDN or CDE is not already a part of your care team. In most cases, appointments with an RDN or CDE are covered by insurance.

WHAT IS AN EATING PATTERN?

"Eating pattern" is simply a term used to describe the foods or groups of foods that a person chooses to eat on a daily basis over time. Examples of eating patterns are vegetarian/vegan, low-carb, low-fat, or Mediterranean-style.

When choosing an eating pattern with your diabetes care team, look for a plan that you feel you can incorporate into your lifestyle and follow long term. It is important for your eating plan to fit your needs, so you can stick to one pattern or implement strategies from a variety of patterns. Remember to take your food likes and dislikes, time constraints, food access, and budget into account as well.

But no matter which eating pattern you choose, there are a few tips you can focus on to make managing your diabetes easier:

- **Eat nonstarchy vegetables**
  - Nonstarchy vegetables are low in calories and carbohydrates and high in essential vitamins and minerals. These include greens (lettuce, spinach, kale, arugula), asparagus, beets, Brussels sprouts, broccoli, cauliflower, carrots, celery, cucumber, mushrooms, onions, peppers, tomatoes, zucchini, and many more.
- **Limit added sugars and refined grains**
  - Added sugars are the sweeteners (such as sugar, corn syrup, brown sugar, honey, maple syrup, and others) added to some foods when they are processed. Added sugars are found in many foods but a few major sources of added sugars include sodas and energy drinks, fruit drinks, baked goods, and candy and desserts (such as ice cream). Refined grains include white or highly processed flours and the products made with them (such as white breads and pastas and many baked goods).
- **Choose whole foods over highly processed foods as often as possible**
  - Whole foods are foods that are as close to their natural form as possible and have had very little processing. Whole foods—such as fresh or frozen fruits and vegetables, beans, whole grains, and fresh meats, poultry, and seafood—provide nutrients that are often removed from processed foods.
- **Choose zero-calorie drinks**
  - If you're thirsty, the best choice is always water. Unsweetened coffee or tea, sparkling water, or flavored waters (made without sugar) are also good choices if you are looking for something more interesting. Try to avoid sugary drinks such as sodas, fruit-flavored drinks, energy drinks, and sweetened coffees and teas.

COMMON EATING PATTERNS
TO HELP MANAGE DIABETES

MEDITERRANEAN-STYLE—This eating pattern emphasizes plant-based foods (vegetables, beans, nuts and seeds, fruits, and whole intact grains), fish and other seafood, and olive oil (which is the main source of fat in this eating pattern). Dairy products, eggs, and wine are included in moderation. Red meat is eaten rarely, as well as sweets, added sugars, and honey. A Mediterranean-style eating pattern may reduce the risk of developing diabetes, and can help lower A1C in people with diabetes. It may also help protect against heart disease and stroke.

VEGETARIAN OR VEGAN—Both of these options are plant-based eating patterns. They are rich in vitamins, minerals, and fiber, and low in fat and cholesterol. People who follow a vegetarian eating pattern do not eat meat, poultry, fish or seafood, though some may choose to eat eggs and/or dairy products. With a vegan eating pattern, all animal products are avoided, including dairy products, eggs, and even honey. Following a vegetarian or vegan eating pattern may help reduce the risk of diabetes, lower A1C, and promote weight loss.

LOW-FAT OR VERY LOW-FAT—These eating patterns emphasize vegetables, fruits, starches (e.g., breads/crackers, pasta, whole grains, and starchy vegetables), lean protein sources, and low-fat dairy products. A low-fat eating pattern is defined as eating less than 30% of your total calories as fat and less than 10% as saturated fat. A very low-fat eating pattern is when a person eats 70–77% carbohydrate (including a lot of fiber), 10% fat, and 13–20% protein per day. A low-fat eating pattern may promote weight loss and reduce the risk of diabetes. A very low-fat eating pattern may also help lower blood pressure.

LOW-CARB OR VERY LOW-CARB—Low-carb eating patterns emphasize vegetables that are low in carbohydrate (also known as nonstarchy vegetables)—such as salad greens, broccoli, cauliflower, cucumber, cabbage, and others. These eating patterns include fat from animal foods, oils, butter, and avocado, and protein in the form of meat, poultry, fish, shellfish, eggs, cheese, nuts, and seeds. People following a low-carb eating pattern avoid starchy and sugary foods such as pasta, rice, potatoes, bread, and sweets. While there is no clear definition of "low-carb," people following this eating pattern generally reduce their carbohydrate intake to 26–45% of their daily calories (low-carb) or less than 26% of their daily calories (very low-carb). Low-carb eating patterns have the potential to reduce A1C, promote weight loss, and lower blood pressure.

DIETARY APPROACHES TO STOP HYPERTENSION (DASH)—This heart-friendly eating pattern emphasizes vegetables, fruits, low-fat dairy products, whole grains, poultry, fish, and nuts. It limits saturated fat, red meat, and sugar-containing foods and beverages. It may also limit sodium. The DASH eating pattern may have the benefit of lowering blood pressure, reducing the risk of diabetes, and promoting weight loss.

With this wide selection of eating patterns available to help manage (or prevent) diabetes, you're sure to find an option that works for you!

WHAT ARE CARBS AND WHY ARE THEY IMPORTANT?

Carbohydrate is a readily used source of energy and the primary dietary influence on blood glucose. A food or drink that contains carbohydrate will have a greater effect on blood glucose than foods that contain protein or fat. Carbohydrate foods can be rich in dietary fiber, vitamins, and minerals and low in added sugars, fats, and sodium, but it is important to focus on the quality of carbohydrate you consume. Fruits, vegetables, beans, and whole grains contain carbohydrates, as do white breads, pastas, and soda. Carbs that come from whole, high-fiber foods are healthier choices than highly processed or sugary foods and drinks. There is not a set amount of carbs that is right for everyone with diabetes to eat each day or at each meal. Reducing total carbs or choosing higher-quality carbs can help with managing blood glucose, but people with diabetes do not need to eliminate or severely restrict carbs to stay healthy. Your carbohydrate intake is a personal decision, which will ideally be based on the personal eating plan that you create with your dietitian or healthcare team. Your healthcare team can help you set carbohydrate goals that are right for you and help you successfully manage diabetes.

WEIGHT LOSS

Weight loss can be helpful for improving blood glucose levels in people with both type 1 and type 2 diabetes and prediabetes. Losing as little as 5% of your body weight can improve diabetes management and reduce your risk for diabetes-related health problems. Strategies for weight loss include changes to your eating behaviors (especially eating fewer calories), regular exercise, or medication and weight-loss surgery. If losing weight is one of your health goals, your healthcare team can help create a weight-loss plan that is safe and appropriate for you.

LOOKING FOR A PLACE TO START?

A good tool to get you started on your journey with diabetes nutrition is the Diabetes Plate Method. If you haven't had a chance to discuss a meal plan with your diabetes care team yet, this meal planning method is an easy way to eat nutritious foods in reasonable portion sizes—and there's no carbohydrate counting or special equipment required! Just start with a 9-inch dinner plate, and fill half of that plate with nonstarchy vegetables (such as salad greens, carrots, broccoli, cauliflower, green beans). Then fill one-quarter of the plate with a protein food (such as chicken, turkey, fish, tofu, etc.), and you can fill the remaining one-quarter with a carb food (such as starchy vegetables like potatoes, grains, fruit, milk, or yogurt). With the Diabetes Plate Method, you can still enjoy your favorite foods (being mindful of portions, of course!) while managing your diabetes.

Breakfast Dishes: Mains and Sides

1

Breakfast Time/Anytime
Lentils and Poached Eggs
page 30

Custard-Cup Frittatas
page 34

Eggs with Tarragon Cream Sauce

SERVES: 4   **SERVING SIZE:** 1 egg, 1 egg white, and 1/4 cup sauce   **HANDS-ON TIME:** 12 minutes
HANDS-OFF TIME: 11 minutes   **TOTAL TIME:** 23 minutes (plus 3 minutes standing time)

This dish can be served as is, over whole-wheat toast or steamed asparagus spears, or on a bed of arugula.

3 cups water, divided
8 eggs
2 cups ice cubes
1/4 tsp salt, divided
1 cup 2% milk
1 Tbsp cornstarch
2 Tbsp light butter with canola oil
1/2 tsp dried tarragon
1/2 tsp Dijon mustard
Black pepper, to taste

1 Place 1 cup of the water in the Instant Pot. Top with a steamer basket. Arrange the eggs in the steamer basket.

2 Seal the lid, close the valve, and set the Manual/Pressure Cook button to 7 minutes.

3 Meanwhile, combine the remaining 2 cups of water with the ice cubes in a medium bowl and place near the Instant Pot.

4 Use a quick pressure release. When the valve drops, carefully remove the lid, remove the steamer basket and eggs. Immediately place the eggs into the bowl of ice water. Let stand for 3 minutes. Peel the eggs, cut them in half, and discard 8 of the egg yolk halves. Slice the remaining eggs, sprinkle with 1/8 tsp salt, and set aside.

5 Combine the milk and cornstarch in a jar, seal the lid, and shake until the cornstarch is dissolved.

6 Discard the water in the pot, press the Cancel button, and reset to Sauté. Then press the Adjust button to "More" or "High." Add the milk mixture to the pot and bring to a boil, stirring frequently. Boil for 2 minutes, or until thickened slightly, stirring frequently. Whisk in the light butter, tarragon, mustard, and remaining 1/8 tsp of salt.

7 Spoon the sauce over the egg slices and sprinkle with pepper to taste.

NUTRITION FACTS

Choices/Exchanges: 1/2 Carbohydrate, 1 Medium-Fat Protein, 1 Fat

Calories: 150; Calories from Fat: 80; Total Fat: 9.0 g; Saturated Fat: 3.3 g; Trans Fat: 0.1 g; Cholesterol: 195 mg; Sodium: 360 mg; Potassium: 220 mg; Total Carbohydrate: 5 g; Dietary Fiber: 0 g; Sugars: 4 g; Protein: 12 g; Phosphorus: 165 mg

Breakfast Time/Anytime Lentils and Poached Eggs

SERVES: 4   **SERVING SIZE:** 3/4 cup lentil mixture and 1 egg   **HANDS-ON TIME:** 13 minutes
HANDS-OFF TIME: About 19 minutes   **TOTAL TIME:** 32 minutes

No need for special silicone cups for this recipe, basic "pyrex-style" ramekins will work in this recipe!

3/4 cup dried brown or green lentils, rinsed and drained
  2 dried bay leaves
  3 cups water, divided
  3 Tbsp extra-virgin olive oil
  1 Tbsp finely chopped fresh parsley
     Grated zest and juice of 1 lemon
1/2 tsp salt, divided
     Nonstick cooking spray
  4 eggs
  4 cups baby spinach
1/4 tsp black pepper

1 Place the lentils, bay leaves, and 2 cups of the water in the Instant Pot. Seal the lid, close the valve, and set the Manual/Pressure Cook button to 7 minutes.

2 Meanwhile, in a small bowl, whisk together the oil, parsley, lemon zest and juice, and 1/4 tsp of the salt. Set aside.

3 Coat 4 (6-oz) ramekins with cooking spray and crack 1 egg into each ramekin. Set aside.

4 Use a quick pressure release. When the valve drops, carefully remove the lid and drain the lentils (discarding the lentil water and 2 bay leaves). Return the lentils to the Instant Pot with the spinach and 1/4 tsp of the salt. Toss until the spinach is just wilted and divide it between 4 soup bowls. Cover to keep warm.

5   Add 1 cup of water to the pot, add a trivet and 3 ramekins. Stack the 4th ramekin on top of the other ramekins. Seal the lid, close the valve, press the Cancel button, and reset the Manual/Pressure Cook button to 1 minute.

6   Use a natural pressure release for 1 minute, followed by a quick pressure release. When the valve drops, carefully remove the lid. Remove the ramekins and drain off any excess water that may have accumulated while cooking. Carefully run a knife around the outer edges of each egg to release from the ramekin easily.

7   Spoon equal amounts of the oil mixture on top of each serving of lentils and top with the eggs. Sprinkle with black pepper.

NUTRITION FACTS

Choices/Exchanges: 1 1/2 Starch, 2 Medium-Fat Protein, 1/2 Fat

Calories: 280; Calories from Fat: 140; Total Fat: 15.0 g; Saturated Fat: 3.0 g; Trans Fat: 0.0 g; Cholesterol: 185 mg; Sodium: 390 mg; Potassium: 590 mg; Total Carbohydrate: 22 g; Dietary Fiber: 9 g; Sugars: 2 g; Protein: 16 g; Phosphorus: 275 mg

Eggs with Hot Pepper Oil

SERVES: 6 **SERVING SIZE:** 2 egg halves and 1 tsp pepper oil **HANDS-ON TIME:** 6 minutes
HANDS-OFF TIME: 11 minutes **TOTAL TIME:** 17 minutes (plus 3 minutes standing time)

This dish is great served for breakfast, as a high protein snack, or served over spring greens for lunch!

3 cups water, divided
6 large eggs
2 cups ice cubes
1 1/2 Tbsp extra-virgin olive oil
2 tsp Sriracha-style hot sauce
1/8 tsp salt

1 Place 1 cup of the water in the Instant Pot. Top with a steamer basket. Arrange the eggs in the steamer basket.

2 Seal the lid, close the valve, and set the Manual/Pressure Cook button to 7 minutes.

3 Meanwhile, combine the remaining 2 cups water with the ice cubes in a medium bowl and place it near the Instant Pot. In a small bowl, stir together the oil, the hot sauce, and the salt.

4 Use a quick pressure release. When the valve drops, carefully remove the lid and place the eggs immediately into the bowl of ice water. Let stand for 3 minutes. Peel the eggs and cut them in half.

5 Place 2 egg halves on each plate and spoon the oil mixture over each serving.

NUTRITION FACTS

Choices/Exchanges: 1 Medium-Fat Protein, 1/2 Fat

Calories: 100; Calories from Fat: 70; Total Fat: 8.0 g; Saturated Fat: 2.0 g;
Trans Fat: 0.0 g; Cholesterol: 185 mg; Sodium: 150 mg; Potassium: 70 mg;
Total Carbohydrate: 1 g; Dietary Fiber: 0 g; Sugars: 1 g; Protein: 7 g;
Phosphorus: 100 mg

Almond Quinoa with Citrus-Zested Strawberries

SERVES: 4   **SERVING SIZE:** A scant 1/2 cup quinoa, 1/3 cup strawberries, and 1/4 cup almonds
HANDS-ON TIME: 9 minutes   **HANDS-OFF TIME:** About 7 minutes   **TOTAL TIME:** 16 minutes

Don't skip the zesting! It adds a huge punch of flavor and heightens the freshness of the berries.

4	oz slivered almonds
1 1/3	cups strawberries, chopped
1	tsp grated orange or lemon zest
2	tsp sugar
1 1/2	cups water, divided
2/3	cup dry organic quinoa (such as Bob's Red Mill)
1/4	tsp salt

1 Press the Sauté button, then press the Adjust button to "More" or "High." When the display says "Hot," add the almonds to the Instant Pot and cook for 2 minutes, or until they begin to lightly brown, stirring occasionally. Place the almonds in a small bowl and set aside.

2 Combine the berries, zest, sugar, and 2 Tbsp water in a medium bowl and set aside.

3 Add the quinoa, salt, and remaining water to the Instant Pot. Seal the lid, close the valve, press the Cancel button, and reset to Manual/Pressure Cook for 2 minutes.

4 Use a quick pressure release. When the valve drops, carefully remove the lid. Divide the quinoa mixture into 4 soup bowls and top with equal amounts of the berry mixture and the almonds.

NUTRITION FACTS

Choices/Exchanges: 1 Starch, 1/2 Fruit, 1/2 Carbohydrate, 1 Lean Protein, 2 1/2 Fat
Calories: 310; Calories from Fat: 150; Total Fat: 17.0 g; Saturated Fat: 1.4 g;
Trans Fat: 0.0 g; Cholesterol: 0 mg; Sodium: 150 mg; Potassium: 450 mg;
Total Carbohydrate: 32 g; Dietary Fiber: 6 g; Sugars: 8 g; Protein: 11 g;
Phosphorus: 280 mg

Custard-Cup Frittatas

SERVES: 4   **SERVING SIZE:** 1 custard cup   **HANDS-ON TIME:** 16 minutes   **HANDS-OFF TIME:** 26 minutes
TOTAL TIME: 42 minutes (plus 5 minutes standing time)

These individual frittatas are packed with veggies and topped with cheddar cheese—and "portion controlled," too! Enjoy these frittatas topped with cheese straight from the ramekin or run a knife around the outer edges, flip them onto a plate, and crown them with cheese. Either way, they're colorful, fun, and very, very satisfying!

Nonstick cooking spray
1 1/3 cups frozen corn kernels, thawed
1 cup chopped kale
1 cup chopped red bell pepper
1 cup finely chopped green onion (both green and white parts)
4 eggs
4 egg whites
1/4 tsp dried thyme
1/4 tsp plus 1/8 tsp salt, divided
4 (6-inch) squares aluminum foil
1 cup water
2 oz grated reduced-fat sharp cheddar cheese

1 Coat 4 (6-oz) ramekins with cooking spray. Divide the corn, kale, bell pepper, and green onion evenly between the ramekins. Press down with the back of a spoon to pack slightly.

2 Whisk together the eggs, egg whites, thyme, and 1/4 tsp salt in a 2-cup measuring cup with a pouring spout or a medium bowl and slowly pour the egg mixture into each ramekin. Coat 4 (6-inch) squares of foil with cooking spray and cover each cup with a sheet of foil, coated side down.

3 Add 1 cup of water to the Instant Pot, add a trivet and 3 ramekins. Stack the 4th ramekin on top of the other ramekins. Seal the lid, close the valve, and set the Manual/Pressure Cook button to 10 minutes.

4   Use a natural pressure release for 10 minutes, followed by a quick pressure release. When the valve drops, carefully remove the lid. Remove the ramekins and carefully remove the foil. Sprinkle the frittatas evenly with the remaining 1/8 tsp salt and the cheese. Let stand for 5 minutes for peak flavors and texture.

NUTRITION FACTS

Choices/Exchanges: 1/2 Starch, 1 Nonstarchy Vegetable, 2 Medium-Fat Protein

Calories: 200; Calories from Fat: 70; Total Fat: 8.0 g; Saturated Fat: 3.1 g; Trans Fat: 0.0 g; Cholesterol: 195 mg; Sodium: 440 mg; Potassium: 410 mg; Total Carbohydrate: 15 g; Dietary Fiber: 3 g; Sugars: 4 g; Protein: 16 g; Phosphorus: 240 mg

Creamy Steel-Cut Oats with Cinnamon and Banana Topping

SERVES: 4   **SERVING SIZE:** 3/4 cup oatmeal, 1/4 cup sliced bananas, and 2 tsp butter mixture
HANDS-ON TIME: 6 minutes   **HANDS-OFF TIME:** About 18 minutes   **TOTAL TIME:** 24 minutes

This recipe calls for cake batter flavored extract, which is a relatively new extract on the shelves. Look for it next to the vanilla and almond extracts. It will give a whole new flavor profile to your bowl of oats!

1 cup steel-cut oats	
3 cups water	
1/4 tsp salt	
2 Tbsp light butter with canola oil	
4 tsp packed brown sugar	
1/2 tsp cake batter flavor or vanilla extract (such as McCormick)	
1/8 tsp ground cinnamon	
1/2 cup 2% milk	
1 cup sliced bananas	

1 Combine the oats, water, and salt in the Instant Pot. Seal the lid, close the valve, and set the Manual/Pressure Cook button to 3 minutes.

2 Use a natural pressure release for 10 minutes, followed by a quick pressure release.

3 Meanwhile, combine the light butter, brown sugar, cake batter flavor, and cinnamon in a small bowl and set aside.

4 When the valve drops, carefully remove the lid. Divide the oatmeal evenly between 4 soup bowls. Top with the milk, spoon the butter mixture in the center, and arrange the bananas around the butter mixture.

NUTRITION FACTS

Choices/Exchanges: 2 Starch, 1/2 Fruit, 1/2 Carbohydrate, 1 Lean Protein
Calories: 260; Calories from Fat: 50; Total Fat: 6.0 g; Saturated Fat: 1.4 g;
Trans Fat: 0.0 g; Cholesterol: 5 mg; Sodium: 210 mg; Potassium: 350 mg;
Total Carbohydrate: 46 g; Dietary Fiber: 5 g; Sugars: 12 g; Protein: 8 g;
Phosphorus: 270 mg

Smoked Sausage, Potato, and Poblano Chop

SERVES: 4   **SERVING SIZE:** 1 cup   **HANDS-ON TIME:** 15 minutes   **HANDS-OFF TIME:** 8 minutes
TOTAL TIME: 23 minutes (plus 10 minutes standing time)

This hearty, "stick-to-your-ribs" dish is great for any time of the day, especially on *cold* days! Because smoked turkey sausages tend to have a lot of sodium per serving, look for products with lower sodium values.

- 2 Tbsp extra-virgin olive oil, divided
- 8 oz smoked turkey sausage, chopped
- 12 oz red potatoes, cut into 1/2-inch cubes
- 8 oz poblano chile peppers, seeded and chopped (about 2 cups total)
- 1/3 cup dry organic quinoa (such as Bob's Red Mill)
- 1 cup water
- 1/2 tsp dried fennel seed
- 1/2 tsp Worcestershire sauce

1. Press the Sauté button, then press the Adjust button to "More" or "High." When the display says "Hot," add 1 Tbsp of the oil and tilt the pot to lightly coat the bottom. Add the sausage and cook for 4 minutes (do *not* stir during this time). Then stir and cook for 1 more minute, or until browned.

2. Add the potatoes, peppers, quinoa, water, fennel seed, and Worcestershire sauce, scraping the bottom of the pot to remove any browned bits.

3. Seal the lid, close the valve, press the Cancel button, and reset to Manual/Pressure Cook for 3 minutes.

4. Use a quick pressure release. When the valve drops, carefully remove the lid. Drizzle with the remaining 1 Tbsp oil. Cover with the lid (do not seal) and let stand for 10 minutes to absorb the flavors.

NUTRITION FACTS

Choices/Exchanges: 1 1/2 Starch, 1/2 Carbohydrate, 1 Medium-Fat Protein, 1 1/2 Fat

Calories: 290; Calories from Fat: 130; Total Fat: 14.0 g; Saturated Fat: 2.7 g; Trans Fat: 0.0 g; Cholesterol: 35 mg; Sodium: 460 mg; Potassium: 700 mg; Total Carbohydrate: 30 g; Dietary Fiber: 5 g; Sugars: 5 g; Protein: 13 g; Phosphorus: 240 mg

Green Chile, Potato, and Black Bean Breakfast Casserole

SERVES: 6   **SERVING SIZE:** 1 wedge (1/6 casserole) plus about 1/3 cup avocado   **HANDS-ON TIME:** 18 minutes
HANDS-OFF TIME: 42 minutes   **TOTAL TIME:** 1 hour (plus 10 minutes standing time)

Here's your new go-to "comfort" recipe with the added bonus of layers of flavors that are still great the next day!

Nonstick cooking spray

6 oz red potatoes, thinly sliced

1 cup shredded reduced-fat sharp cheddar cheese, divided

1/2 (15-oz) can no-salt-added black beans, rinsed and drained

1 tsp ground cumin

1/2 cup chopped green onion (both green and white parts)

1 (4-oz) can chopped hot green chilies

4 large eggs

2 egg whites

1/2 tsp salt

1 cup water

1 (18-inch-long) sheet aluminum foil

2 avocados, peeled and chopped

1 lime, cut into 6 wedges

1. Coat a 7-inch nonstick springform pan with cooking spray. Arrange the potatoes on the bottom of the pan, and top with 1/2 cup of the cheese, the beans, cumin, green onion, and chilies.

2. In a medium bowl, whisk together the eggs, egg whites, and salt; pour evenly over the ingredients in the pan. Wrap the pan completely in foil. Seal tightly.

3. Place the water and a trivet in the Instant Pot.

4. Make a foil sling by folding an 18-inch-long piece of foil in half lengthwise. Place the springform pan in the center of the sling and lower the pan into the pot. Fold down the excess foil from the sling to allow the lid to close properly.

5   Seal the lid, close the valve, and set the Manual/Pressure Cook button to 27 minutes.

6   Use a natural pressure release for 10 minutes, followed by a quick pressure release. When the valve drops, carefully remove the lid. Remove the pan using the sling. Blot off any excess moisture that is on the foil before removing. Sprinkle with the remaining cheese. Let stand for 10 minutes to allow the cheese to melt and the casserole to firm up slightly.

7   Remove the sides of the pan. Cut into 6 wedges, top with avocado, and serve with the lime wedges to squeeze over all.

NUTRITION FACTS

Choices/Exchanges: 1/2 Starch, 1/2 Fruit, 2 Medium-Fat Protein, 1 Fat

Calories: 250; Calories from Fat: 140; Total Fat: 15.0 g; Saturated Fat: 4.1 g; Trans Fat: 0.0 g; Cholesterol: 135 mg; Sodium: 470 mg; Potassium: 600 mg; Total Carbohydrate: 18 g; Dietary Fiber: 6 g; Sugars: 2 g; Protein: 14 g; Phosphorus: 260 mg

Buttery Raisin Apples

SERVES: 4   **SERVING SIZE:** 1 apple half   **HANDS-ON TIME:** 10 minutes   **HANDS-OFF TIME:** 6 minutes
TOTAL TIME: 16 minutes (plus 5 minutes standing time)

The actual cooking time for this recipe is only 1 minute! The hard part is waiting for it while it stands for 5 minutes after cooking to absorb those sweet and buttery flavors. But it is definitely worth the wait!

1   cup water
2   (8-oz) apples (such as Gala), halved and cored
1   Tbsp raisins
1/2 tsp grated orange zest
1/4 tsp ground nutmeg
1   Tbsp light butter with canola oil
2   tsp packed brown sugar
1/2 tsp vanilla extract

1 Place the water and a steamer basket in the Instant Pot. Place apples in the steamer basket, cut side up.

2 In a small bowl, combine the raisins, orange zest, and nutmeg. Stir until well blended. Fill the cavity in each apple with equal amounts of the raisin mixture.

3 Seal the lid, close the valve, and set the Manual/Pressure Cook button to 1 minute.

4 Use a quick pressure release. When the valve drops, carefully remove the lid. Remove apples.

5 In the same small bowl used for the raisin mixture, combine the remaining ingredients, stirring until well blended. Top apples with equal amounts of the butter mixture and let stand for 5 minutes to allow the butter to melt and the apples to absorb the flavors.

NUTRITION FACTS

Choices/Exchanges: 1 Fruit, 1/2 Fat

Calories: 80; Calories from Fat: 15; Total Fat: 1.5 g; Saturated Fat: 0.6 g; Trans Fat: 0.0 g; Cholesterol: 2 mg; Sodium: 25 mg; Potassium: 135 mg; Total Carbohydrate: 19 g; Dietary Fiber: 3 g; Sugars: 15 g; Protein: 0 g; Phosphorus: 15 mg

Protein, Veggie, and Grain Main Dish Salads

2

Chicken Curry Salad on Asparagus, Edamame, and Greens

page 44

Wheat Berry, Black Bean, and Avocado Salad
page 47

Chicken Curry Salad on Asparagus, Edamame, and Greens

SERVES: 4   **SERVING SIZE:** About 1/2 cup chicken mixture, 1/2 cup asparagus mixture, and 1 cup kale
HANDS-ON TIME: 12 minutes   **HANDS-OFF TIME:** 23 minutes   **TOTAL TIME:** 35 minutes

You can always serve curry salad by itself or on a bed of lettuce, but you can bump up the fiber (a lot) and make it so much more interesting with *very* little effort using this recipe!

- 12 oz boneless, skinless chicken breast
- 1 tsp ground cumin
- 1/4 tsp black pepper
- 2 cups water
- 1/4 cup plain 2% Greek yogurt (such as Fage)
- 1/4 cup light mayonnaise
- 1 Tbsp sugar
- 1 1/2 tsp curry powder
- 1/2 tsp salt
- 2 cups cut asparagus, about 1-inch pieces
- 1 cup fresh or frozen shelled edamame, thawed
- 4 cups baby kale mix (such as Dole Power Up Greens)
- 1/2 cup chopped red onion
- 1/4 cup chopped fresh cilantro or green onion

1 Sprinkle the chicken with the cumin and pepper. Place the water and a steamer basket in the Instant Pot. Arrange the chicken in the steamer basket. Seal the lid, close the valve, and set the Manual/Pressure Cook button to 6 minutes.

2 Use a natural pressure release for 5 minutes, followed by a quick pressure release. When the valve drops, carefully remove the lid. Remove the chicken and place it on a cutting board. Let stand for 5 minutes before shredding. Set aside.

3 Meanwhile, whisk together the yogurt, mayonnaise, sugar, curry, and salt in a medium bowl and set aside.

4 Place the asparagus and edamame in the steamer basket in the pot. Seal the lid, close the valve, press the Cancel button, and reset to Manual/Pressure Cook for 1 minute.

5 Use a quick pressure release. Transfer the asparagus mixture to a colander. Run it under cold water to stop the cooking process and cool quickly; drain well.

6 Place equal amounts of the kale mix on each of 4 dinner plates. Top with equal amounts of the asparagus mixture.

7 Add the chicken and onions to the yogurt mixture and toss until well coated. Spoon equal amounts on top of each serving of the asparagus mixture, and sprinkle with cilantro.

NUTRITION FACTS

Choices/Exchanges: 1/2 Carbohydrate, 2 Nonstarchy Vegetable, 3 Lean Protein, 1/2 Fat

Calories: 240; Calories from Fat: 70; Total Fat: 8.0 g; Saturated Fat: 1.4 g; Trans Fat: 0.0 g; Cholesterol: 50 mg; Sodium: 470 mg; Potassium: 660 mg; Total Carbohydrate: 17 g; Dietary Fiber: 5 g; Sugars: 8 g; Protein: 26 g; Phosphorus: 285 mg

Chickpea–Kale Salad with Pepperoni

SERVES: 4   **SERVING SIZE:** About 1 3/4 cups   **HANDS-ON TIME:** 12 minutes   **HANDS-OFF TIME:** 48 minutes
TOTAL TIME: 1 hour

Most of the "Hands-On" activity for this recipe can be done while the chickpeas are under pressure. So get the peas under pressure and then prep the rest! Then all you have to do is rinse the chickpeas and toss it all together! Be sure to shred or thinly slice the kale instead of serving it chopped to get an interesting and refreshing texture. It's much more fun to eat that way!

6	oz dried chickpeas, rinsed and drained
3	cups water
1	dried bay leaf
2	cups shredded or thinly sliced kale
1	cucumber, chopped
1/3	cup chopped red onion
2	avocados, peeled and chopped
1 1/2	oz crumbled reduced-fat blue cheese
1	oz turkey pepperoni slices, quartered
2	Tbsp white balsamic vinegar
1	Tbsp extra-virgin olive oil
1/4	tsp salt

1 Combine the chickpeas, water, and bay leaf in the Instant Pot. Seal the lid, close the valve, and set the Manual/Pressure Cook button to 30 minutes.

2 Use a natural pressure release for 10 minutes, followed by a quick pressure release. When the valve drops, carefully remove the lid. Remove the chickpeas to a colander and drain. Run under cold water to stop the cooking process and cool quickly. Drain well; remove and discard the bay leaf.

3 Combine the chickpeas with the remaining ingredients and serve.

NUTRITION FACTS

Choices/Exchanges: 2 Starch, 1/2 Fruit, 1 Nonstarchy Vegetable, 1 Lean Protein, 3 Fat

Calories: 390; Calories from Fat: 180; Total Fat: 20.0 g; Saturated Fat: 4.0 g; Trans Fat: 0.0 g; Cholesterol: 15 mg; Sodium: 470 mg; Potassium: 940 mg; Total Carbohydrate: 41 g; Dietary Fiber: 12 g; Sugars: 9 g; Protein: 16 g; Phosphorus: 265 mg

Wheat Berry, Black Bean, and Avocado Salad

SERVES: 4   **SERVING SIZE:** 1 1/2 cups   **HANDS-ON TIME:** 12 minutes   **HANDS-OFF TIME:** 35 minutes
TOTAL TIME: 47 minutes

What's a wheat berry? It is a whole-wheat kernel composed of the bran, germ, and endosperm of wheat. In other words, it's the edible portion—the *whole* wheat kernel without the outer shell. They are available in major supermarkets and health food stores. In addition to being high in nutrients, they taste great and make for a great conversation starter with your friends!

2 oz dried black beans
1/2 cup hard wheat berries
4 cups water
1 (10-oz) container grape tomatoes, halved
1 cup chopped poblano chile peppers
1/2 cup chopped fresh cilantro
2 Tbsp cider vinegar
2 Tbsp extra-virgin olive oil
1 garlic clove, minced
1/2 tsp salt
1 avocado, peeled and chopped
3/4 cup shredded reduced-fat sharp cheddar cheese

1 Place the beans and wheat berries in a fine mesh sieve; rinse and drain. Place in the Instant Pot with the water. Seal the lid, close the valve, and set the Manual/Pressure Cook button to 25 minutes.

2 Use a quick pressure release. Meanwhile, combine the tomatoes, peppers, cilantro, vinegar, oil, garlic, and salt in a large bowl and set aside.

3 When the valve drops, carefully remove the lid. Drain the beans and wheat berries in a fine mesh sieve. Run under cold water to stop the cooking process and cool quickly. Drain well.

4 Combine the drained bean mixture, avocado, and cheese with the tomato mixture. Toss gently until well coated and serve.

COOK'S NOTE
This flavorful, nutritious salad can be served over Bibb lettuce, if desired.

NUTRITION FACTS

Choices/Exchanges: 1 1/2 Starch, 1 Nonstarchy Vegetable, 1 Lean Protein, 3 Fat

Calories: 320; Calories from Fat: 150; Total Fat: 17.0 g; Saturated Fat: 4.1 g; Trans Fat: 0.0 g; Cholesterol: 15 mg; Sodium: 440 mg; Potassium: 650 mg; Total Carbohydrate: 31 g; Dietary Fiber: 9 g; Sugars: 4 g; Protein: 13 g; Phosphorus: 285 mg;

Sweet Tarragon Egg and Asparagus Salad with Avocado

SERVES: 4   **SERVING SIZE:** About 2 cups salad and 1 1/2 Tbsp dressing   **HANDS-ON TIME:** 12 minutes
HANDS-OFF TIME: 23 minutes   **TOTAL TIME:** 35 minutes

This is not your typical egg salad! It goes way beyond the ordinary and explodes with flavor, texture, and a refreshing combination of ingredients. Have you ever tried "white" or "golden" balsamic vinegar? It's sold right next to the traditional variety, but gives a sweetness and lightness to the vinegar. Once you've tried it, you'll be hooked! The dressing for this salad is very pungent, so a little goes a long way!

- 4 cups water, divided
- 4 large eggs
- 2 cups ice cubes
- 1/4 cup white balsamic vinegar
- 1 Tbsp sugar
- 1 Tbsp canola oil
- 1/2 tsp dried tarragon
- 1/2 tsp salt, divided
- 8 oz asparagus, cut into 2-inch pieces
- 4 cups baby kale mix (such as Dole Power Up Greens)
- 4 slices ultra-thin Swiss cheese, cut into very thin strips (about 2 oz total)
- 1 avocado, peeled and chopped

1 Place 2 cups of the water in the Instant Pot. Top with a steamer basket. Arrange the eggs in the steamer basket. Seal the lid, close the valve, and set the Manual/Pressure Cook button to 7 minutes.

2 Meanwhile, combine the remaining 2 cups of water with the ice cubes in a medium bowl and place near the Instant Pot.

3 Combine the balsamic vinegar, sugar, oil, tarragon, and 1/4 tsp of the salt in a small bowl and whisk until well blended.

4 Use a quick pressure release. When the valve drops, carefully remove the lid. Remove the eggs with tongs or a large spoon and immediately place in the ice water. Let stand for 3 minutes before peeling and cutting the eggs into quarters.

5 Place the asparagus in the steamer basket in the pot. Seal the lid, close the valve, and press the Cancel button. Reset to Manual/Pressure Cook for 1 minute.

6 Use a quick pressure release. When the valve drops, carefully remove the lid. Remove the asparagus and the steamer basket and run it under cold water to stop the cooking process and cool quickly. Drain well.

7 Divide the kale mix evenly among 4 dinner plates. Top with the cheese, asparagus, avocado, and eggs. Sprinkle evenly with the remaining 1/4 tsp of salt. Spoon the dressing evenly over all. Do not stir.

NUTRITION FACTS

Choices/Exchanges: 1/2 Carbohydrate, 1 Nonstarchy Vegetable, 2 Medium-Fat Protein, 1 1/2 Fat

Calories: 270; Calories from Fat: 160; Total Fat: 18.0 g; Saturated Fat: 4.9 g; Trans Fat: 0.1 g; Cholesterol: 200 mg; Sodium: 400 mg; Potassium: 510 mg; Total Carbohydrate: 16 g; Dietary Fiber: 5 g; Sugars: 9 g; Protein 13 g; Phosphorus 255 mg

Green Bean and Feta Pasta Salad

SERVES: 4   **SERVING SIZE:** 1 1/2 cups   **HANDS-ON TIME:** 12 minutes   **HANDS-OFF TIME:** 8 minutes
TOTAL TIME: 20 minutes

You can serve this salad now or serve it tomorrow! If serving the next day, just add an additional teaspoon or two of the cider vinegar before serving to "brighten" the flavors.

- 4 oz uncooked multigrain rotini pasta (such as Barilla Protein Plus)
- 2 cups fresh green beans, trimmed (about 6 oz total), broken into 2-inch pieces
- 4 cups water
- 2 Tbsp extra-virgin olive oil, divided
- 1 cup packed fresh baby spinach
- 1/2 cup chopped red onion
- 12 pitted kalamata olives, coarsely chopped
- 3 oz crumbled reduced-fat feta cheese
- 1 1/2 Tbsp cider vinegar
- 1 tsp dried oregano
- 1/8 tsp crushed pepper flakes

1 Combine the pasta, green beans, water, and 1 tsp of the oil in the Instant Pot. Stir, making sure the pasta is covered by the water. Seal the lid, close the valve, and set the Manual/Pressure Cook button to 3 minutes.

2 Use a quick pressure release. When the valve drops, carefully remove the lid. Drain into a colander. Run under cold water to stop the cooking process and cool quickly. Drain well.

3 Meanwhile, combine the remaining ingredients in a large bowl. Add the pasta and green bean mixture and toss gently until just blended.

NUTRITION FACTS

Choices/Exchanges: 1 Starch, 1 Nonstarchy Vegetable, 1 Lean Protein, 2 Fat

Calories: 250; Calories from Fat: 120; Total Fat: 13.0 g; Saturated Fat: 2.6 g; Trans Fat: 0.0 g; Cholesterol: 10 mg; Sodium: 420 mg; Potassium: 330 mg; Total Carbohydrate: 26 g; Dietary Fiber: 5 g; Sugars: 3 g; Protein: 11 g; Phosphorus: 180 mg

Ginger, Lentil, and Goat Cheese Salad

SERVES: 4   **SERVING SIZE:** 1 1/4 cups   **HANDS-ON TIME:** 12 minutes   **HANDS-OFF TIME:** 13 minutes
TOTAL TIME: 25 minutes (plus 30 minutes chill time)

Take a break from your typical grain or bean salads. This dish serves up some personality! It's full of freshly grated ginger and creamy goat cheese with a splash of lemon!

3/4 cup dried brown or green lentils, rinsed
2 cups water
1/2 tsp ground allspice
1 cup chopped carrots
1 cup chopped cucumber
1/2 cup chopped fresh cilantro or fresh parsley
1/3 cup chopped red onion
1/2 tsp salt, divided
2 Tbsp canola oil
3 Tbsp cider vinegar
2 tsp grated fresh ginger
1/8 tsp crushed pepper flakes
4 oz crumbled goat cheese
1 lemon, cut into 4 wedges

1 Combine the lentils, water, and allspice in the Instant Pot. Seal the lid, close the valve, and set the Manual/Pressure Cook button to 5 minutes.

2 Use a quick pressure release. When the valve drops, carefully remove the lid. Add the carrots, cover (do not lock), and let stand for 2 minutes. Drain the lentils and carrots in a colander. Run under cold water to stop the cooking process and cool quickly. Drain well.

3 Place the lentils and carrots in a large bowl with the cucumber, cilantro, onion, and 1/4 tsp of salt.

4 Whisk together the oil, vinegar, ginger, remaining 1/4 tsp of salt, and pepper flakes in a small bowl. Add to the lentil mixture and toss gently until well blended. Top with the goat cheese.

5 Cover the salad and refrigerate for 30 minutes. Serve with the lemon wedges to squeeze over all.

COOK'S NOTE
Be sure to squeeze the lemon juice over the salad at the time of serving to give it a splash of "freshness" and bring up the flavors of the dish!

NUTRITION FACTS

Choices/Exchanges: 1 1/2 Starch, 1 Nonstarchy Vegetable, 1 Lean Protein, 2 Fat

Calories: 290; Calories from Fat: 130; Total Fat: 14.0 g; Saturated Fat: 4.8 g; Trans Fat: 0.0 g; Cholesterol: 30 mg; Sodium: 420 mg; Potassium: 580 mg; Total Carbohydrate: 29 g; Dietary Fiber: 10 g; Sugars: 5 g; Protein 15 g; Phosphorus: 265 mg

Rosemary, Shrimp, and Potato Salad on Greens

SERVES: 4   **SERVING SIZE:** About 2 1/2 cups   **HANDS-ON TIME:** 13 minutes   **HANDS-OFF TIME:** 17 minutes
TOTAL TIME: 30 minutes (plus 1 hour chill time)

Hot outside? Here's an easy and much needed make-ahead entrée salad for patio entertaining, brown bag lunches, and, well, any time to help get you through those hot summers!

1	cup water
1 1/2	lb petite potatoes, quartered
12	oz peeled raw shrimp*
3/4	cup chopped red onion
1/4	cup extra-virgin olive oil
1/4	cup red wine vinegar
1	tsp dried rosemary
1	garlic clove, minced
1/4	tsp crushed pepper flakes
4	cups kale mix (such as Dole Power Up Greens)
1/2	tsp salt
1	cup grape tomatoes, halved

1 Place the water in the Instant Pot. Top with a steamer basket. Arrange the potatoes in the steamer basket. Seal the lid, close the valve, and set the Manual/Pressure Cook button to 3 minutes.

2 Use a quick pressure release. When the valve drops, carefully remove the lid.

3 Add the shrimp in with the potatoes. Seal the lid, close the valve, and press the Cancel button. Reset to Manual/Pressure Cook for 1 minute.

*If possible, use fresh (never frozen) shrimp or shrimp that are free of preservatives (for example, shrimp that have not been treated with salt or STPP [sodium tripolyphosphate]).

4   Use a quick pressure release. When the valve drops, carefully remove the lid. Immediately remove the shrimp and potatoes from the pot and place in a large bowl with the onion, oil, vinegar, rosemary, garlic, and pepper flakes. Toss very gently and refrigerate for 1 hour, stirring occasionally.

5   Place equal amounts of the kale mix on each of 4 dinner plates. Add the salt to the shrimp mixture and toss gently. Spoon equal amounts of the shrimp mixture on top of the kale; arrange the tomatoes around the outer edges of each serving.

NUTRITION FACTS

Choices/Exchanges: 2 Starch, 1 Nonstarchy Vegetable, 2 Lean Protein, 1 1/2 Fat

Calories: 340; Calories from Fat: 130; Total Fat: 14.0 g; Saturated Fat: 2.0 g; Trans Fat: 0.0 g; Cholesterol: 100 mg; Sodium: 400 mg; Potassium: 1350 mg; Total Carbohydrate: 37 g; Dietary Fiber: 5 g; Sugars: 5 g; Protein: 19 g; Phosphorus: 245 mg

Farro–Lentil Warm Salad Bowls

SERVES: 4   **SERVING SIZE:** About 1 1/2 cups   **HANDS-ON TIME:** 12 minutes   **HANDS-OFF TIME:** 13 minutes
TOTAL TIME: 25 minutes

Cooking grains and legumes together for the same dish will shorten the already short cooking time; you don't have to cook them separately. Just check your unit's cooking directions for timing. If the times for the two ingredients are similar, it will work for you!

1/2	cup uncooked pearled farro
1/2	cup dried brown or green lentils, rinsed and drained
4	cups water
1 1/2	Tbsp extra-virgin olive oil
1	tsp grated lemon zest
1/2	tsp salt
1/4	tsp black pepper
2	cups packed baby spinach or baby greens (such as kale mix)
1 1/2	oz crumbled reduced-fat blue cheese
1/4	cup raisins
2	oz chopped walnuts

1 Combine the farro, lentils, and water in the Instant Pot. Seal the lid, close the valve, and set the Manual/Pressure Cook button to 7 minutes.

2 Use a quick pressure release. When the valve drops, carefully remove the lid. Drain the farro and lentils in a fine mesh sieve. Run under cold water to stop the cooking process and cool quickly. Drain well.

3 Combine the farro mixture with the oil, lemon zest, salt, and pepper. Toss until well blended. Divide the mixture evenly into 4 shallow bowls. Arrange the remaining ingredients in sections on top of the farro mixture.

NUTRITION FACTS

Choices/Exchanges: 2 Starch, 1/2 Fruit, 1 Lean Protein, 3 Fat

Calories: 360; Calories from Fat: 150; Total Fat: 17.0 g; Saturated Fat: 3.0 g; Trans Fat: 0.0 g; Cholesterol: 5 mg; Sodium: 460 mg; Potassium: 630 mg; Total Carbohydrate: 41 g; Dietary Fiber: 10 g; Sugars: 7 g; Protein: 15 g; Phosphorus: 310 mg

Sandwiches: Open-Faced, Wrapped, Stuffed, and Between the Bun

3

Minted Moroccan Chicken Wraps
page 60

**Avocado Toasts
with Egg**
page 64

Diner-Style Smothered Chicken on Whole-Wheat Bread

SERVES: 4   **SERVING SIZE:** 3 oz cooked chicken, about 1/2 cup pea mixture, and 1 bread slice
HANDS-ON TIME: 10 minutes   **HANDS-OFF TIME:** 23 minutes   **TOTAL TIME:** 33 minutes

If you're old enough to remember the dime store and drugstore diners, you'll have a flash back to those days when you bite into these hot, open-face sandwiches. If not, you're in for a treat . . . and a new hot sandwich favorite!

 1 cup water, divided
 2 (8-oz) boneless, skinless chicken breasts
 2 packets sodium-free granulated chicken bouillon (2 tsp)
 1 tsp dried thyme
1/2 tsp onion powder
1/4 tsp plus 1/8 tsp salt, divided
1 1/2 cups chopped red bell pepper
1 1/2 Tbsp cornstarch
 1 cup frozen green peas
1/2 cup chopped green onion (both green and white parts)
 4 (1-oz) slices whole-wheat bread
     Black pepper, to taste

1 Place all but 2 Tbsp of the water in the Instant Pot. Top with the chicken, sprinkle with the bouillon, thyme, onion powder, and 1/8 tsp of the salt. Top with the bell pepper.

2 Seal the lid, close the valve, and set the Manual/Pressure Cook button to 5 minutes.

3 Use a natural pressure release for 5 minutes, followed by a quick pressure release. When the valve drops, carefully remove the lid. Remove the chicken with a slotted spoon (leaving the peppers in the pot) and place the chicken on a cutting board. Let the chicken stand for 5 minutes before thinly slicing.

4 Meanwhile, combine the remaining 2 Tbsp of water with the cornstarch in a small bowl. Stir until the cornstarch is dissolved.

5 Press the Cancel button and set to Sauté. Then press the Adjust button to "More" or "High." Bring to a boil, and stir in the cornstarch mixture, frozen peas, and green onion. Return to a boil and boil for 2 minutes, stirring frequently, to thicken slightly and cook the peas.

6 Remove the pot insert from the Instant Pot. Stir in the remaining 1/4 tsp of salt.

7 Place the sliced chicken on top of the bread slices (dividing evenly between the slices), top with the pea mixture, and sprinkle with pepper.

NUTRITION FACTS

Choices/Exchanges: 1 1/2 Starch, 1 Nonstarchy Vegetable, 3 Lean Protein

Calories: 260; Calories from Fat: 35; Total Fat: 4.0 g; Saturated Fat: 1.0 g; Trans Fat: 0.0 g; Cholesterol: 65 mg; Sodium: 440 mg; Potassium: 690 mg; Total Carbohydrate: 25 g; Dietary Fiber: 5 g; Sugars: 6 g; Protein: 30 g; Phosphorus: 280 mg

Minted Moroccan Chicken Wraps

SERVES: 6   **SERVING SIZE:** 1/3 cup chicken mixture, 1/4 cup yogurt mixture, and 1 tortilla
HANDS-ON TIME: 12 minutes   **HANDS-OFF TIME:** 30 minutes   **TOTAL TIME:** 42 minutes

Don't underestimate the power of fresh herbs. They add a tremendous amount of freshness and are calorie-free!

- 1 cup roasted red peppers, drained
- 1 tsp ground coriander
- 1 tsp ground cumin
- 1 tsp garlic powder
- 1/2 tsp ground chipotle pepper
- 1/2 tsp caraway seeds
- 1/2 cup water
- 1 lb boneless, skinless chicken thighs, trimmed of fat
- 1/4 tsp salt
- 3/4 cup plain 2% Greek yogurt (such as Fage)
- 1/2 cup chopped fresh mint
- 1/3 cup finely chopped red onion
- 6 light flour tortillas (such as La Tortilla Factory Light Tortillas), heated in a skillet until slightly charred
- 1 lemon, cut into 6 wedges

1. Combine the peppers, coriander, cumin, garlic powder, chipotle, caraway, and water in a blender. Secure the lid and purée until smooth.

2. Place the chicken thighs in the Instant Pot. Top with the puréed pepper mixture. Seal the lid, close the valve, and set the Manual/Pressure Cook button to 10 minutes.

3. Use a natural pressure release for 10 minutes, followed by a quick pressure release. When the valve drops, carefully remove the lid. Remove the chicken with a slotted spoon and place on a cutting board. Let the chicken stand for 5 minutes before shredding.

4   Press the Cancel button and set to Sauté. Then press the Adjust button to "More" or "High." Bring to a boil and boil for 5 minutes to thicken slightly. Stir the chicken and salt into the sauce.

5   In a medium bowl, combine the yogurt, mint, and onion. Spoon the yogurt mixture evenly over each tortilla, squeeze the lemon wedges over each serving, and top with equal amounts of the chicken mixture. Fold the edges of the tortillas over or serve open face with a knife and fork, if desired.

NUTRITION FACTS

Choices/Exchanges: 1 Starch, 1 Nonstarchy Vegetable, 2 Lean Protein, 1/2 Fat
Calories: 210; Calories from Fat: 60; Total Fat: 7.0 g; Saturated Fat: 2.5 g;
Trans Fat: 0.0 g; Cholesterol: 70 mg; Sodium: 460 mg; Potassium: 360 mg;
Total Carbohydrate: 23 g; Dietary Fiber: 7 g; Sugars: 5 g; Protein: 20 g;
Phosphorus: 250 mg

Little Turkey Tortillas

SERVES: 4   **SERVING SIZE:** 2/3 cup turkey mixture, 2 tortillas, 2 Tbsp onion, and 2 Tbsp cheese
HANDS-ON TIME: 15 minutes   **HANDS-OFF TIME:** 12 minutes   **TOTAL TIME:** 27 minutes

Handheld and fun to eat, these turkey tortillas are easy to fix for "the big game" or a "movie-in" night!

Nonstick cooking spray
1 lb 97% lean ground turkey
1/2 (15-oz) can no-salt-added black beans, rinsed and drained
2 tsp smoked paprika
2 tsp ground cumin
1/8 tsp plus 1/4 tsp salt, divided
1 cup water
2 Tbsp tomato paste
8 (6-inch) corn tortillas
1/2 cup finely chopped red onion
2 oz shredded reduced-fat sharp cheddar cheese

1 Press the Sauté button, then press the Adjust button to "More" or "High." When the display says "Hot," coat the Instant Pot with cooking spray. Add the turkey and cook for 4 minutes, or until browned, stirring occasionally.

2 Stir in the beans, paprika, cumin, 1/8 tsp of the salt, and the water. Seal the lid, close the valve, press the Cancel button, and set to Manual/Pressure Cook for 5 minutes.

3 Use a quick pressure release. Meanwhile, preheat your broiler.

4 When the valve drops, carefully remove the lid. Stir in the tomato paste, press the Cancel button, and reset to Sauté. Then press the Adjust button to "More" or "High." Bring to a boil and boil for 4 minutes, or until thickened.

5 Stir in the remaining 1/4 tsp of salt. Turn off the heat.

6 Place the tortillas in a single layer on 2 baking sheets. Top each tortilla with equal amounts of turkey mixture, onions, and cheese. Place 1 baking sheet under the broiler and broil for 1 minute, watching closely so the cheese doesn't burn. Remove and repeat with the remaining baking sheet.

NUTRITION FACTS

Choices/Exchanges: 2 Starch, 1 Nonstarchy Vegetable, 4 Lean Protein

Calories: 370; Calories from Fat: 70; Total Fat: 8.0 g; Saturated Fat: 2.8 g; Trans Fat: 0.0 g; Cholesterol: 75 mg; Sodium: 400 mg; Potassium: 700 mg; Total Carbohydrate: 38 g; Dietary Fiber: 6 g; Sugars: 3 g; Protein: 37 g; Phosphorus: 525 mg

Fish Fast Wraps

SERVES: 4   **SERVING SIZE:** About 2 oz cooked fish, 1 cup lettuce, 1 tortilla, and 2 Tbsp sauce
HANDS-ON TIME: 11 minutes   **HANDS-OFF TIME:** 7 minutes   **TOTAL TIME:** 18 minutes

This recipe needs exactly 2 minutes under pressure, unless your fish fillets are more than 3/4 inches thick, in which case the fish will take 3 minutes! Either way, have everything ready before you start cooking because it goes fast!

1 cup plus 1 Tbsp water, divided
10 oz cod fillets, about 1/2 inch thick
1/3 cup plain 2% Greek yogurt (such as Fage)
2 Tbsp light mayonnaise
4 tsp capers
1 tsp dried dill
4 light flour tortillas (such as La Tortilla Factory Light Tortillas), warmed
4 cups shredded romaine
1/4 cup chopped red onion
1/16 tsp salt
1/4 tsp black pepper
1 lemon, cut into 4 wedges

1 Place 1 cup of the water in the Instant Pot and top with a steamer basket. Arrange the fish in the steamer basket. Seal the lid, close the valve, and set the Manual/Pressure Cook button to 2 minutes.

2 Use a quick pressure release. Meanwhile, combine the yogurt, mayonnaise, capers, remaining 1 Tbsp of water, and the dill in a small bowl. Using a fork, mash the capers into the other ingredients and stir until well blended. Set aside.

3 When the valve drops, carefully remove the lid. Remove the steamer basket and fish from the pot.

4 Top each tortilla with equal amounts of the romaine, onion, and sauce. Flake the fish into large pieces, sprinkle with the salt and pepper, and place the fish on top of the sauce. Serve with the lemon wedges to squeeze over all.

NUTRITION FACTS

Choices/Exchanges: 1 Starch, 1/2 Carbohydrate, 2 Lean Protein

Calories: 190; Calories from Fat: 45; Total Fat: 5.0 g; Saturated Fat: 1.5 g; Trans Fat: 0.0 g; Cholesterol: 35 mg; Sodium: 470 mg; Potassium: 370 mg; Total Carbohydrate: 21 g; Dietary Fiber: 7 g; Sugars: 3 g; Protein: 19 g; Phosphorus: 205 mg

Avocado Toasts with Egg

SERVES: 4   **SERVING SIZE:** 3 thin slices toast (1 oz total), 6 Tbsp avocado mixture, 1 egg white, 2 Tbsp tomato, 1 Tbsp cilantro, 1 1/2 tsp onion   **HANDS-ON TIME:** 15 minutes
HANDS-OFF TIME: 11 minutes   **TOTAL TIME:** 26 minutes (plus 3 minutes standing time)

Most of the "Hands-On" activity for this recipe happens while the eggs are cooking and cooling, cutting down on the total time. Nice!

3 cups water, divided
4 large eggs
2 cups ice cubes
2 avocados, peeled and roughly mashed
1 jalapeño, seeded (if desired) and minced
3 Tbsp light mayonnaise
3 Tbsp lemon juice
1 tsp Dijon mustard
1/4 tsp salt
4 oz multigrain Italian loaf bread, cut diagonally into 12 **thin** slices and lightly toasted
1/2 cup diced tomato
1/4 cup chopped fresh cilantro
2 Tbsp minced red onion
1 lemon, cut into 4 wedges

1 Place 1 cup of the water into the Instant Pot. Top with a steamer basket. Arrange the eggs in the steamer basket. Seal the lid, close the valve, and set the Manual/Pressure Cook button to 7 minutes.

2 Meanwhile, combine the remaining 2 cups of water with the ice cubes in a medium bowl and place near the Instant Pot.

3 In a small bowl, stir together the mashed avocado, jalapeño, mayonnaise, lemon juice, mustard, and salt.

4 Use a quick pressure release. When the valve drops, carefully remove the lid and place the eggs immediately into the ice water. Let stand for 3 minutes.

5 Peel the eggs and cut the eggs in half, discarding 4 of the egg yolk halves. Add the remaining egg yolk halves to the avocado mixture and mash until well blended (it will be slightly lumpy). Finely chop all of the egg whites and set aside.

6 Spread the avocado mixture on bread slices (dividing it evenly between the slices) and top with the chopped egg whites, tomato, cilantro, and onion. Serve with the lemon wedges to squeeze over all.

NUTRITION FACTS

Choices/Exchanges: 1 Starch, 1/2 Fruit, 1 Lean Protein, 3 Fat

Calories: 280; Calories from Fat: 150; Total Fat: 17.0 g; Saturated Fat: 2.9 g; Trans Fat: 0.0 g; Cholesterol: 95 mg; Sodium: 450 mg; Potassium: 600 mg; Total Carbohydrate: 24 g; Dietary Fiber: 8 g; Sugars: 5 g; Protein: 11 g; Phosphorus: 170 mg

Middle Eastern Spiced Beef Pitas with Raisins

SERVES: 4   **SERVING SIZE:** 3/4 cup beef mixture and 1/2 pita bread   **HANDS-ON TIME:** 13 minutes
HANDS-OFF TIME: 18 minutes   **TOTAL TIME:** 31 minutes

Pull out the napkins! These overstuffed pitas are scrumptious and a bit on the messy side. They're so fun!

	Nonstick cooking spray
12	oz extra-lean (95% lean) ground beef
2	oz slivered almonds
1 1/2	cups frozen peppers and onions
1	tsp dried thyme
1	tsp ground cinnamon
1/2	tsp ground cumin
1/4	tsp ground allspice
1/4	tsp crushed pepper flakes
1/4	tsp plus 1/8 tsp salt, divided
1	cup water
1/3	cup raisins
1/4	cup tomato paste
2	whole-wheat pita bread, cut in half and warmed

1 Press the Sauté button, then press the Adjust button to "More" or "High." When the display says "Hot," coat the Instant Pot with cooking spray. Add the beef and almonds and cook for 4 minutes, or until beef is browned. Add the frozen pepper mixture, thyme, cinnamon, cumin, allspice, pepper flakes, 1/8 tsp of the salt, and the water. Top with the raisins. Do not stir.

2 Seal the lid, close the valve, and set the Manual/Pressure Cook button to 10 minutes.

3 Use a quick pressure release. When the valve drops, carefully remove the lid. Stir in the tomato paste, press the Cancel button, and reset to Sauté. Then press the Adjust button to "More" or "High." Bring to a boil and boil for 2 minutes, or until thickened slightly, stirring frequently. Stir in the remaining 1/4 tsp of salt.

4 Spoon equal amounts of the beef mixture into the pita halves and serve.

NUTRITION FACTS

Choices/Exchanges: 1 Starch, 1/2 Fruit, 1/2 Carbohydrate, 1 Nonstarchy Vegetable, 3 Lean Protein, 1 Fat

Calories: 330; Calories from Fat: 120; Total Fat: 13.0 g; Saturated Fat: 2.6 g; Trans Fat: 0.1 g; Cholesterol: 50 mg; Sodium: 430 mg; Potassium: 710 mg; Total Carbohydrate: 34 g; Dietary Fiber: 6 g; Sugars: 11 g; Protein: 24 g; Phosphorus: 305 mg

Spiced-and-Sloppy Sloppy Joes

SERVES: 8   **SERVING SIZE:** 1/2 cup beef mixture and 1 bun   **HANDS-ON TIME:** 16 minutes
HANDS-OFF TIME: 11 minutes   **TOTAL TIME:** 27 minutes

Sloppy Joes are named "sloppy" for a reason! This sloppy joe recipe gives new meaning to the name while packing in tons of flavor and veggies, too!

Nonstick cooking spray
1 lb extra-lean (95% lean) ground beef
1 cup chopped red bell pepper
8 oz sliced mushrooms
3/4 cup matchstick carrots
1 (10-oz) can tomatoes with mild chilies (such as Ro-Tel)
1/2 cup water
2 Tbsp balsamic vinegar
1/2 tsp ground cinnamon
1/2 tsp ground cumin
1/4 cup tomato paste
2 tsp sugar
8 whole-wheat hamburger buns, warmed

1 Press the Sauté button, then press the Adjust button to "More" or "High." When the display says "Hot," coat the Instant Pot with cooking spray. Add the beef and cook for 3 minutes, or until browned. Add the bell peppers, mushrooms, carrots, tomatoes, water, vinegar, cinnamon, and cumin.

2 Seal the lid, close the valve, press the Cancel button, and reset to Manual/Pressure Cook for 5 minutes.

3 Use a quick pressure release. When the valve drops, carefully remove the lid. Stir in the tomato paste. Press the Cancel button and reset to Sauté. Then press the Adjust button to "More" or "High." Add the sugar, bring to a boil and boil for 5 minutes, or until thickened slightly, stirring frequently.

4 Spoon 1/2 cup of the beef mixture on each hamburger bun and serve.

COOK'S NOTE

This recipe freezes well. Be sure to freeze any leftovers in individual portions so they're easy to thaw and reheat. Plus this makes it easier to control your portion!

NUTRITION FACTS

Choices/Exchanges: 1 1/2 Starch, 1 Nonstarchy Vegetable, 2 Lean Protein

Calories: 230; Calories from Fat: 45; Total Fat: 5.0 g; Saturated Fat: 1.7 g; Trans Fat: 0.1 g; Cholesterol: 35 mg; Sodium: 380 mg; Potassium: 600 mg; Total Carbohydrate: 30 g; Dietary Fiber: 5 g; Sugars: 9 g; Protein: 17 g; Phosphorus: 245 mg

Shredded Pork with Sweet–Hot Sriracha BBQ Dressing

SERVES: 12   **SERVING SIZE:** 1/2 cup pork mixture and 1 Tbsp sauce   **HANDS-ON TIME:** 12 minutes
HANDS-OFF TIME: 1 hour and 25 minutes   **TOTAL TIME:** 1 hour and 37 minutes

There are so many ways to enjoy this dish! You can serve the pork and sauce in lettuce wraps, on corn tortillas, or on top of baked potatoes or sweet potatoes! You can try it over carrot veggie spirals, too! On top of that, the pork and sauce freeze well. It's best to freeze them in separate containers, though.

2 lb trimmed, boneless pork shoulder, cut into 4 pieces*	**1** Place the pork in the Instant Pot, top with the frozen pepper mixture, wine, water, oregano, paprika, and pepper.
4 cups frozen peppers and onions	**2** Seal the lid, close the valve, and set the Manual/Pressure Cook button to 75 minutes.
1 cup dry white wine	**3** Use a quick pressure release. Meanwhile, combine the barbecue sauce, mayonnaise, and hot sauce in a small bowl.
1/2 cup water	
2 tsp dried oregano	
1 tsp paprika	**4** When the valve drops, carefully remove the lid. Place a colander over a bowl and drain the pork mixture, reserving 1/3 cup of the cooking liquid. Shred the pork and return it to the pot with the drained vegetable mixture, the reserved 1/3 cup of liquid, and the salt. Stir until well blended.
1/2 tsp black pepper	
1/2 cup barbecue sauce (such as Sweet Baby Ray's)	
1/4 cup light mayonnaise	**5** Serve on buns, if desired, and top with sauce.
2 tsp Sriracha-style hot sauce	
1/2 tsp salt	

*When purchasing beef or pork, always buy about 8 oz more than you need. You will lose some of the weight after the meat is trimmed of fat.

NUTRITION FACTS

Choices/Exchanges: 1/2 Carbohydrate, 2 Lean Protein, 1 Fat

Calories: 180; Calories from Fat: 80; Total Fat: 9.0 g; Saturated Fat: 2.9 g; Trans Fat: 0.0 g; Cholesterol: 55 mg; Sodium: 290 mg; Potassium: 260 mg; Total Carbohydrate: 8 g; Dietary Fiber: 0 g; Sugars: 6 g; Protein: 15 g; Phosphorus: 140 mg

Soups, Stews, and Anything in a Bowl

4

Coconut Curry Vegetable Rice Bowls

page 77

Freezer-Fix Chili
page 74

Mexican Chicken and Fresh Tomato Soup

SERVES: 6   **SERVING SIZE:** 1 cup chicken mixture plus about 1/3 cup avocado   **HANDS-ON TIME:** 11 minutes
HANDS-OFF TIME: 26 minutes   **TOTAL TIME:** 37 minutes

This is a "minimal chop" kind of soup, which means that the only things that need to be chopped are the cilantro and avocado. It's jam-packed with the flavors of Mexico—totally jam-packed!

- 8 oz boneless, skinless chicken thighs, trimmed of fat
- 1 (15-oz) can hominy, rinsed and drained
- 1 (15-oz) can no-salt-added black beans, rinsed and drained
- 1 (10-oz) container grape tomatoes
- 1 (4-oz) can chopped hot green chilies
- 1 cup water
- 2 tsp ground cumin
- 1 tsp paprika
- 1/2 cup chopped fresh cilantro
- 2 Tbsp extra-virgin olive oil
- 1/2 tsp salt
- 2 avocados, peeled and chopped
- 1 lime, cut into 4 wedges

1 Combine the chicken, hominy, beans, tomatoes, green chilies, water, cumin, and paprika in the Instant Pot.

2 Seal the lid, close the valve, and set the Manual/Pressure Cook button to 8 minutes.

3 Use a natural pressure release for 10 minutes, followed by a quick pressure release. When the valve drops, carefully remove the lid. Remove the chicken, shred it. and return it to the pot. Stir the mixture to break up the tomatoes. Stir in the cilantro, oil, and salt.

4 Serve topped evenly with the avocado. Serve with the lime wedges to squeeze over all.

NUTRITION FACTS

Choices/Exchanges: 1 Starch, 1/2 Carbohydrate, 2 Lean Protein, 2 Fat

Calories: 280; Calories from Fat: 130; Total Fat: 14.0 g; Saturated Fat: 2.2 g; Trans Fat: 0.0 g; Cholesterol: 35 mg; Sodium: 380 mg; Potassium: 720 mg; Total Carbohydrate: 27 g; Dietary Fiber: 8 g; Sugars: 4 g; Protein: 14 g; Phosphorus: 205 mg

White Bean and Sausage Bowls

SERVES: 4   **SERVING SIZE:** About 1 1/4 cups   **HANDS-ON TIME:** 18 minutes   **HANDS-OFF TIME:** 42 minutes
TOTAL TIME: 1 hour (plus 1 hour standing time)

Sometimes, don't you just feel like you need a hot bowl of comfort? This recipe should help! Enjoy rich, browned smoked sausage cooked with big fat white beans, cabbage, carrots, and herbs and served in a thick mug or bowl. It's warm and hearty!

Nonstick cooking spray
6 oz smoked turkey sausage, thinly sliced*
4 oz dried large white beans, rinsed and drained
2 1/2 cups water
2 cups coarsely chopped cabbage
1 cup frozen sliced carrots
1 cup chopped celery
1 cup chopped onion
1/2 tsp dried thyme
1 dried bay leaf
1/8 tsp black pepper
1/8 tsp salt
1 Tbsp extra-virgin olive oil

*Because smoked turkey sausages tend to have a lot of sodium per serving, look for products with lower sodium values.

1 Press the Sauté button, then press the Adjust button to "More" or "High." When the display says "Hot," coat the Instant Pot with cooking spray. Add the sausage and cook for 4 minutes, or until browned, stirring occasionally.

2 Stir in the beans and water. Top with the remaining ingredients, except the oil. Do not stir, but make sure the beans are covered by the other ingredients.

3 Seal the lid, close the valve, press the Cancel button, and set to Manual/Pressure Cook for 25 minutes.

4 Use a natural pressure release for 10 minutes, followed by a quick pressure release. When the valve drops, carefully remove the lid. Stir in the oil. Discard the bay leaf before serving. If time allows, let stand for 1 hour (or more) before serving.

> **COOK'S NOTE**
> This dish tastes even better the next day!

NUTRITION FACTS

Choices/Exchanges: 1 Starch, 3 Nonstarchy Vegetable, 1 Lean Protein, 1 Fat
Calories: 240; Calories from Fat: 80; Total Fat: 9.0 g; Saturated Fat: 1.8 g;
Trans Fat: 0.0 g; Cholesterol: 25 mg; Sodium: 460 mg; Potassium: 870 mg;
Total Carbohydrate: 30 g; Dietary Fiber: 8 g; Sugars: 7 g; Protein: 15 g;
Phosphorus: 205 mg

Freezer-Fix Chili

SERVES: 6   **SERVING SIZE:** 1 cup chili   **HANDS-ON TIME:** 5 minutes   **HANDS-OFF TIME:** 35 minutes
TOTAL TIME: 40 minutes

Start with a package of ground turkey that's frozen hard as a rock and before you know it, you have a delicious chili!

1	lb frozen 93% lean ground turkey
1 1/2	cups frozen corn, divided
1	(15-oz) can no-salt-added black beans, rinsed and drained, divided
1	(14.5-oz) can no-salt-added diced tomatoes
1	cup water
2	Tbsp chili powder
1	Tbsp ground cumin
1 1/2	tsp smoked paprika
3/4	tsp salt

1 Place the frozen ground turkey in the Instant Pot and top with the remaining ingredients, reserving 1/3 cup of the corn and 1/3 cup of the black beans for garnish.

2 Seal the lid, close the valve, and set the Manual/Pressure Cook button to 25 minutes.

3 Use a quick pressure release. When the valve drops, carefully remove the lid and stir, breaking up the turkey.

4 Before serving, garnish each portion with the reserved corn (thawed) and black beans.

COOK'S NOTE

Top each serving of this chili with a little cilantro before serving, if desired.

NUTRITION FACTS

Choices/Exchanges: 1 Starch, 1 Nonstarchy Vegetable, 2 Lean Protein, 1/2 Fat
Calories: 220; Calories from Fat: 60; Total Fat: 7.0 g; Saturated Fat: 1.8 g;
Trans Fat: 0.1 g; Cholesterol: 55 mg; Sodium: 400 mg; Potassium: 640 mg;
Total Carbohydrate: 22 g; Dietary Fiber: 5 g; Sugars: 4 g; Protein: 20 g;
Phosphorus: 265 mg

Lentils with Smoked Sausage and Fennel

SERVES: 4   **SERVING SIZE:** About 1 1/4 cups   **HANDS-ON TIME:** 11 minutes   **HANDS-OFF TIME:** 26 minutes
TOTAL TIME: 37 minutes

Dried fennel is used here to intensify the heartiness and "meatiness" of the sausage without overloading the dish with saturated fat and sodium.

Nonstick cooking spray
5 oz smoked turkey sausage, diced*
3/4 cup dried brown or green lentils, rinsed and drained
2 cups frozen peppers and onions
3 cups water
3 packets sodium-free granulated chicken bouillon (1 Tbsp)
2 Tbsp extra-virgin olive oil
2 tsp dried oregano
1 tsp smoked paprika
1 tsp hot sauce (such as Frank's RedHot)
1/2 tsp dried fennel
1/3 cup chopped fresh parsley
1/4 tsp salt

1 Press the Sauté button, then press the Adjust button to "More" or "High." When the display says "Hot," coat the Instant Pot with cooking spray. Add the sausage and cook for 4 minutes, or until browned, stirring occasionally.

2 Stir in the lentils, frozen pepper mixture, water, bouillon, oil, oregano, paprika, hot sauce, and fennel. Seal the lid, close the valve, press the Cancel button, and set to Manual/Pressure Cook for 10 minutes.

3 Use a natural pressure release for 10 minutes, followed by a quick pressure release. When the valve drops, carefully remove the lid. Stir in the parsley and salt and serve.

*Because smoked turkey sausages tend to have a lot of sodium per serving, look for products with lower sodium values.

NUTRITION FACTS

Choices/Exchanges: 1 1/2 Starch, 1 Nonstarchy Vegetable, 1 Lean Protein, 1 1/2 Fat

Calories: 260; Calories from Fat: 110; Total Fat: 12.0 g; Saturated Fat: 2.0 g; Trans Fat: 0.0 g; Cholesterol: 25 mg; Sodium: 480 mg; Potassium: 830 mg; Total Carbohydrate: 27 g; Dietary Fiber: 9 g; Sugars: 5 g; Protein: 15 g; Phosphorus: 240 mg

Chipotle White Bean Soup with Cilantro

SERVES: 6   **SERVING SIZE:** 1 cup soup   **HANDS-ON TIME:** 10 minutes   **HANDS-OFF TIME:** 1 hour
TOTAL TIME: 1 hour and 10 minutes

Don't forget, you can always use fresh veggies instead of frozen in my recipes! But using frozen veggies really does cut down on the prep time, and that comes in handy when you're in a hurry and/or your energy levels are low. It works for me!

- 6 oz dried navy beans, rinsed and drained
- 2 cups water
- 1 (14.5-oz) can no-salt-added diced tomatoes
- 2 cups frozen sliced carrots
- 1 cup chopped celery
- 1 cup chopped onion
- 1 Tbsp minced chipotle chile pepper (canned in adobo sauce; about 1 large pepper)
- 3 packets sodium-free granulated chicken bouillon (1 Tbsp)
- 1 Tbsp ground cumin, divided
- 1/2 cup chopped fresh cilantro
- 2 Tbsp extra-virgin olive oil
- 1 tsp salt
- 1 tsp sugar
- 1 lime, cut into 6 wedges

1 Combine the beans, water, tomatoes, carrots, celery, onion, chipotle chilies, bouillon, and 2 tsp of the cumin in the Instant Pot.

2 Seal the lid, close the valve, and set the Manual/Pressure Cook button to 45 minutes.

3 Use a quick pressure release. When the valve drops, carefully remove the lid, stir in the remaining 1 tsp of cumin and all the remaining ingredients, except the lime. Serve with the lime wedges to squeeze over all.

NUTRITION FACTS

Choices/Exchanges: 1 Starch, 2 Nonstarchy Vegetable, 1 Fat

Calories: 190; Calories from Fat: 50; Total Fat: 6.0 g; Saturated Fat: 0.7 g; Trans Fat: 0.0 g; Cholesterol: 0 mg; Sodium: 470 mg; Potassium: 910 mg; Total Carbohydrate: 29 g; Dietary Fiber: 7 g; Sugars: 7 g; Protein: 8 g; Phosphorus: 160 mg

Coconut Curry Vegetable Rice Bowls

SERVES: 6   **SERVING SIZE:** 1 cup   **HANDS-ON TIME:** 13 minutes   **HANDS-OFF TIME:** 32 minutes
TOTAL TIME: 45 minutes

Preparing curries often involves a lot of chopping, but you can get around that easily. Take advantage of the pre-chopped or no-salt-added canned ingredients on the market, such as matchstick carrots, water chestnuts, and chickpeas. They're ready and waiting for you!

2/3 cup uncooked brown rice, rinsed and drained
1 cup water
1 tsp curry powder
3/4 tsp salt, divided
1 cup chopped green onion (both green and white parts)
1 cup sliced red or yellow bell pepper
1 cup matchstick carrots
1 cup chopped red or purple cabbage
1 (8-oz) can sliced water chestnuts, drained
1 (15-oz) can no-salt-added chickpeas, rinsed and drained
1 (13-oz) can lite coconut milk
1 Tbsp grated fresh ginger
1 1/2 Tbsp sugar

1 Combine the rice, water, curry powder, and 1/4 tsp of the salt in the Instant Pot.

2 Seal the lid, close the valve, and set the Manual/Pressure Cook button to 15 minutes.

3 Use a natural pressure release for about 12 minutes. When the valve drops, carefully remove the lid and stir in the remaining ingredients.

4 Press the Cancel button and set to Sauté. Then press the Adjust button to "More" or "High." Bring to a boil and boil for 2 minutes, or until all the ingredients are heated through, stirring occasionally.

NUTRITION FACTS

Choices/Exchanges: 2 Starch, 2 Nonstarchy Vegetable, 1 Fat

Calories: 240; Calories from Fat: 50; Total Fat: 6.0 g; Saturated Fat: 3.5 g; Trans Fat: 0.0 g; Cholesterol: 0 mg; Sodium: 330 mg; Potassium: 540 mg; Total Carbohydrate: 42 g; Dietary Fiber: 7 g; Sugars: 9 g; Protein: 8 g; Phosphorus: 230 mg

Spicy Thai Mushroom Soup with Chickpeas

SERVES: 4   **SERVING SIZE:** 1 1/2 cups   **HANDS-ON TIME:** 10 minutes   **HANDS-OFF TIME:** 16 minutes
TOTAL TIME: 26 minutes (plus 5 minutes standing time)

If you can't stand the heat, just cut back on the hot sauce, and serve it alongside the dish for those who can't get enough of it! Either way, don't skip this recipe—it is *so so so* good!

8 oz sliced mushrooms (preferably baby portobellos)
2 cups frozen peppers and onions
1 (15-oz) can no-salt-added chickpeas, rinsed and drained
1 (14.5-oz) can no-salt-added diced tomatoes
1/2 cup water
1 Tbsp Sriracha-style hot sauce, or to taste
1/2 tsp ground cumin
1 1/2 cups lite coconut milk
1/2 cup chopped fresh cilantro
1 Tbsp sugar
1 Tbsp grated fresh ginger
1/2 tsp salt

1 Combine the mushrooms, frozen pepper mixture, chickpeas, tomatoes, water, hot sauce, and cumin in the Instant Pot.

2 Seal the lid, close the valve, and set the Manual/Pressure Cook button to 8 minutes.

3 Use a quick pressure release. When the valve drops, carefully remove the lid and stir in the remaining ingredients. Let stand for 5 minutes to absorb the flavors.

NUTRITION FACTS

Choices/Exchanges: 1 Starch, 1/2 Carbohydrate, 2 Nonstarchy Vegetable, 1 Lean Protein, 1 Fat

Calories: 240; Calories from Fat: 60; Total Fat: 7.0 g; Saturated Fat: 4.8 g; Trans Fat: 0.0 g; Cholesterol: 0 mg; Sodium: 440 mg; Potassium: 930 mg; Total Carbohydrate: 35 g; Dietary Fiber: 7 g; Sugars: 13 g; Protein: 12 g; Phosphorus: 305 mg

Louisiana Shrimp Bowls

SERVES: 6   **SERVING SIZE:** About 1 1/2 cups   **HANDS-ON TIME:** 12 minutes   **HANDS-OFF TIME:** 27 minutes
TOTAL TIME: 39 minutes

A cross between a gumbo and a creole, this "one dish" meal contains plenty of okra. It's a Southern dish for sure!

- 4 cups frozen cut okra
- 2 cups frozen peppers and onions
- 1 cup frozen corn kernels
- 1 1/2 cups chopped celery
- 1 (14.5-oz) can no-salt-added diced tomatoes
- 1/2 cup water
- 1 1/2 tsp dried thyme
- 1 tsp sugar
- 1/8 tsp cayenne pepper
- 12 oz peeled raw shrimp*
- 1 crookneck yellow squash, chopped
- 1 cup chopped green onion (both green and white parts)
- 1 tsp seafood seasoning (such as Old Bay)
- 2 Tbsp extra-virgin olive oil
- 1 1/2 tsp hot sauce (such as Frank's RedHot)
- 1/2 tsp salt

1 Combine the okra, frozen pepper mixture, corn, celery, tomatoes, water, thyme, sugar, and cayenne in the Instant Pot.

2 Seal the lid, close the valve, and set the Manual/Pressure Cook button to 3 minutes.

3 Use a quick pressure release. When the valve drops, carefully remove the lid and stir in the shrimp, squash, green onion, and seafood seasoning.

4 Seal the lid, close the valve, press the Cancel button, and reset the Manual/Pressure Cook button to 1 minute.

5 Use a quick pressure release. When the valve drops, carefully remove the lid and stir in the oil, hot sauce, and salt. Even better the next day.

*If possible, use fresh (never frozen) shrimp or shrimp that are free of preservatives (for example, shrimp that have not been treated with salt or STPP [sodium tripolyphosphate]).

NUTRITION FACTS

Choices/Exchanges: 1/2 Starch, 3 Nonstarchy Vegetable, 1 Lean Protein, 1/2 Fat

Calories: 180; Calories from Fat: 45; Total Fat: 5.0 g; Saturated Fat: 0.8 g; Trans Fat: 0.0 g; Cholesterol: 105 mg; Sodium: 480 mg; Potassium: 720 mg; Total Carbohydrate: 19 g; Dietary Fiber: 5 g; Sugars: 7 g; Protein: 17 g; Phosphorus: 225 mg

Tomato and Kalamata Cod Bowls

SERVES: 4 **SERVING SIZE:** 1 cup fish mixture plus about 1/2 cup rice **HANDS-ON TIME:** 11 minutes
HANDS-OFF TIME: 16 minutes **TOTAL TIME:** 27 minutes (plus 5 minutes standing time)

Fresh tomatoes—tiny sweet grape tomatoes—are plopped in the pot with tomato sauce, wine, Greek olives, and basil, pressure-cooked briefly, and then combined with the remaining ingredients. Cook for 2 more minutes and that's it—that is it!

1 (10-oz) container grape tomatoes
1 cup diced onion
1 (8-oz) can no-salt-added tomato sauce
1/4 cup dry white wine
16 pitted kalamata olives, coarsely chopped
1 Tbsp extra-virgin olive oil
1 Tbsp dried basil
1/4 tsp crushed pepper flakes
2 Tbsp tomato paste
12 oz cod fillets, cut into 1-inch chunks
1/2 cup no-salt-added navy or cannellini beans, rinsed and drained
1/8 tsp salt
1 (8.8-oz) package cooked whole-grain rice (such as Uncle Ben's Ready Rice)
3 Tbsp grated Parmesan cheese

1 Combine the tomatoes, onion, tomato sauce, wine, olives, oil, basil, and pepper flakes in the Instant Pot. Seal the lid, close the valve, and set the Manual/Pressure Cook button to 3 minutes.

2 Use a quick pressure release. When the valve drops, carefully remove the lid and stir in the tomato paste until well blended. Stir in the fish, beans, and salt. Seal the lid, close the valve, press the Cancel button, and reset the Manual/Pressure Cook button to 2 minutes.

3 Use a quick pressure release. When the valve drops, carefully remove the lid. Turn off the heat. Gently stir and let stand, uncovered, for 5 minutes to absorb the flavors. (For a thinner consistency, add 1/2 cup of water at the end of cooking time.)

4 Prepare the rice according to package directions. Spoon the fish mixture over the rice and top with the cheese.

NUTRITION FACTS

Choices/Exchanges: 1 1/2 Starch, 3 Nonstarchy Vegetable, 2 Lean Protein, 1 Fat
Calories: 320; Calories from Fat: 100; Total Fat: 11.0 g; Saturated Fat: 1.3 g;
Trans Fat: 0.0 g; Cholesterol: 40 mg; Sodium: 430 mg; Potassium: 950 mg;
Total Carbohydrate: 36 g; Dietary Fiber: 7 g; Sugars: 7 g; Protein: 23 g;
Phosphorus: 335 mg

Potato and Corn Fish Chowder

SERVES: 4   **SERVING SIZE:** 1 1/2 cups   **HANDS-ON TIME:** 15 minutes   **HANDS-OFF TIME:** 20 minutes
TOTAL TIME: 35 minutes (plus 10 minutes standing time)

Using frozen fish? Great! Partially thaw the fish under cold running water and then cut it up. When the fish is just partially frozen, it is easier to cut!

8 oz russet potatoes, chopped
2 cups chopped onions
2 cups frozen corn kernels
2 dried bay leaves
1 cup water
12 oz tilapia or flounder fillets, cut into 1-inch pieces
1/4 tsp cayenne pepper
1 cup 2% milk
2 tsp Worcestershire sauce
2 Tbsp light butter with canola oil
1/2 tsp salt
2 Tbsp chopped fresh parsley

1 Combine the potatoes, onions, corn, bay leaves, and water in the Instant Pot. Seal the lid, close the valve, and set the Manual/Cook Pressure button to 3 minutes.

2 Use a quick pressure release. When the valve drops, carefully remove the lid and stir in the fish and cayenne.

3 Seal the lid, close the valve, press the Cancel button, and reset the Manual/Pressure Cook button to 2 minutes.

4 Use a quick pressure release. When the valve drops, carefully remove the lid. Stir in the remaining ingredients, except the parsley. Turn off the heat. Let stand for 10 minutes to absorb the flavors. Remove and discard bay leaves before serving. Garnish with the parsley.

> **COOK'S NOTE**
> For a thicker consistency, use a potato masher and lightly mash the mixture.

NUTRITION FACTS

Choices/Exchanges: 1 1/2 Starch, 2 Nonstarchy Vegetable, 2 Lean Protein, 1/2 Fat
Calories: 280; Calories from Fat: 50; Total Fat: 6.0 g; Saturated Fat: 2.4 g;
Trans Fat: 0.1 g; Cholesterol: 50 mg; Sodium: 450 mg; Potassium: 880 mg;
Total Carbohydrate: 35 g; Dietary Fiber: 4 g; Sugars: 9 g; Protein: 23 g;
Phosphorus: 310 mg

Beef, Beer, and Bean Chili Bowls

SERVES: 6   **SERVING SIZE:** 1 cup chili   **HANDS-ON TIME:** 13 minutes   **HANDS-OFF TIME:** 55 minutes
TOTAL TIME: 1 hour and 8 minutes (plus 10 minutes standing time)

For a fun twist and "fuller" bowl, top the chili with shredded lettuce before you add the sour cream and onions!

Nonstick cooking spray
- 12 oz extra-lean (95% lean) ground beef
- 4 oz dried pinto beans, rinsed and drained
- 4 cups frozen peppers and onions
- 1 (14.5-oz) can no-salt-added diced tomatoes
- 1 1/2 Tbsp chili powder
- 1 Tbsp ground cumin
- 2 tsp smoked paprika
- 12 oz can light beer (such as Miller Lite)
- 1/2 cup water
- 1 Tbsp sugar
- 1 Tbsp extra-virgin olive oil
- 3/4 tsp salt
- 6 Tbsp light sour cream
- 6 Tbsp finely chopped green onion (both green and white parts)

1 Press the Sauté button, then press the Adjust button to "More" or "High." When the display says "Hot," coat the Instant Pot with cooking spray. Add the beef and cook for 4 minutes, or until browned, stirring occasionally. Stir in the beans, frozen pepper mixture, tomatoes, chili powder, cumin, paprika, beer, and water.

2 Seal the lid, close the valve, press the Cancel button, and reset to Manual/Pressure Cook for 40 minutes.

3 Use a quick pressure release. When the valve drops, carefully remove the lid.
Stir in the sugar, oil, and salt. Let stand for 10 minutes to absorb the flavors.

4 Serve topped with sour cream and green onion.

> **COOK'S NOTE**
>
> This chili is even better the next day. Top with the sour cream and green onion just before serving.

NUTRITION FACTS

Choices/Exchanges: 1 Starch, 2 Nonstarchy Vegetable, 2 Lean Protein, 1/2 Fat

Calories: 250; Calories from Fat: 60; Total Fat: 7.0 g; Saturated Fat: 2.7 g; Trans Fat: 0.1 g; Cholesterol: 40 mg; Sodium: 400 mg; Potassium: 740 mg; Total Carbohydrate: 24 g; Dietary Fiber: 5 g; Sugars: 7 g; Protein: 18 g; Phosphorus: 235 mg

Hot 'n Cold Appetizers and Snacks

5

Stuffed Petite Peppers
page 96

Smoky White Bean Hummus

SERVES: 7   **SERVING SIZE:** 1/4 cup hummus   **HANDS-ON TIME:** 10 minutes   **HANDS-OFF TIME:** 50 minutes
TOTAL TIME: 1 hour

Hummus, of course, is a good old standby when you want an easy snack or appetizer, but don't limit yourself—think outside the dip! You can use hummus as a protein on crispbread or in tortilla wraps, or fill a pita pocket with this protein powerhouse. Just 1/4 cup of this hummus provides 5 grams of protein!

- 4 cups water
- 3/4 cup dried navy beans, rinsed and drained
- 3 garlic cloves, peeled
- 1 tsp smoked paprika
- 1/8 tsp cayenne pepper
- 2–3 Tbsp lime juice
- 1/2 tsp ground cumin
- 3/4 tsp salt
- 2 Tbsp extra-virgin olive oil

1 Combine the water, beans, and garlic in the Instant Pot.

2 Seal the lid, close the valve, and set the Manual/Pressure Cook button to 30 minutes.

3 Use a natural pressure release for 10 minutes, followed by a quick pressure release. When the valve drops, carefully remove the lid. Place a colander over a bowl and drain the beans, reserving 1/2 cup of the cooking liquid.

4 Place the drained bean mixture, the 1/2 cup of reserved liquid, the smoked paprika, cayenne, lime juice, cumin, and salt in a blender. Secure the lid, holding it down firmly, and purée until smooth. Place in a bowl and stir in the oil.

COOK'S NOTE

You can serve this with fresh veggies, such as red pepper strips, petite sweet peppers, sugar snap peas, snow peas, or grape tomatoes. Use wooden toothpicks for dipping!

NUTRITION FACTS

Choices/Exchanges: 1 Starch, 1 Lean Protein

Calories: 110; Calories from Fat: 40; Total Fat: 4.5 g; Saturated Fat: 0.6 g; Trans Fat: 0.0 g; Cholesterol: 0 mg; Sodium: 250 mg; Potassium: 280 mg; Total Carbohydrate: 15 g; Dietary Fiber: 4 g; Sugars: 1 g; Protein 5 g; Phosphorus: 95 mg

Hot Spinach Dip with Rosemary Wheat Crackers

SERVES: 16   **SERVING SIZE:** 1/4 cup dip plus 4 crackers   **HANDS-ON TIME:** 15 minutes
HANDS-OFF TIME: About 15 minutes   **TOTAL TIME:** 30 minutes

Serving a crowd? This creamy dip is loaded with spinach, artichokes, and cheese. Serve it with herbed crackers to balance out the flavors in every single bite!

Nonstick cooking spray
1 cup chopped onion
1 (10-oz) package frozen chopped spinach
1 (9-oz) package frozen artichoke hearts
1 1/2 tsp dried oregano
1 cup water
4 oz reduced-fat cream cheese, cut into small pieces
1/4 tsp cayenne pepper, or to taste
1/2 tsp salt
4 oz shredded reduced-fat sharp cheddar cheese
64 rosemary whole-wheat crackers (such as Triscuit)

1 Press the Sauté button, then press the Adjust button to "More" or "High." When the display says "Hot," coat the Instant Pot with cooking spray. Add the onion and cook for 4 minutes, or until translucent, stirring frequently. Add the frozen spinach, frozen artichoke hearts, oregano, and water.

2 Seal the lid, close the valve, press the Cancel button, and reset to Manual/Pressure Cook for 6 minutes.

3 Use a quick pressure release. When the valve drops, carefully remove the lid. Stir in the cream cheese, cayenne pepper, and salt. Stir until the cream cheese has melted completely, breaking down the artichokes while stirring. Add the cheddar cheese and stir until melted.

4 Serve with crackers.

NUTRITION FACTS

Choices/Exchanges: 1 Starch, 1 Nonstarchy Vegetable, 1 Fat

Calories: 140; Calories from Fat: 50; Total Fat: 6.0 g; Saturated Fat: 2.1 g;
Trans Fat: 0.0 g; Cholesterol: 10 mg; Sodium: 260 mg; Potassium: 200 mg;
Total Carbohydrate: 17 g; Dietary Fiber: 4 g; Sugars: 2 g; Protein: 6 g;
Phosphorus: 135 mg

Minted Split Pea Dip

SERVES: 8   **SERVING SIZE:** About 3 Tbsp dip   **HANDS-ON TIME:** 10 minutes   **HANDS-OFF TIME:** 20 minutes
TOTAL TIME: 30 minutes

This is a refreshing veggie dip, but you can try it as a filling for lettuce bundles and wraps or use it as a sandwich spread, too! Pile it high with crisp veggies!

- 6 oz dried split green peas, rinsed and drained
- 3 cups water
- 2 Tbsp extra-virgin olive oil, divided
- 1/4 cup chopped fresh mint
- 2 tsp grated lemon zest
- 2 Tbsp lemon juice
- 1 garlic clove, peeled
- 3/4 tsp salt
- 1/8 tsp cayenne pepper

1 Combine the peas, water, and 1 1/2 tsp of the oil in the Instant Pot. Seal the lid, close the valve, and set the Manual/Pressure Cook button to 12 minutes.

2 Use a quick pressure release. When the valve drops, carefully remove the lid. Drain the pea mixture in a fine mesh sieve, reserving 1/4 cup of the cooking liquid. Rinse under cold water and drain well.

3 Place the peas and reserved 1/4 cup of liquid in a blender with the mint, lemon zest, lemon juice, garlic, salt, and cayenne. Secure the lid, holding it down firmly, and purée until smooth. Place in a bowl and stir in the remaining oil.

4 Serve with veggies—such as cucumber spears, green bell pepper strips, and celery—and with lemon wedges, if desired.

NUTRITION FACTS

Choices/Exchanges: 1 Starch, 1/2 Fat

Calories: 100; Calories from Fat: 30; Total Fat: 3.5 g; Saturated Fat: 0.5 g; Trans Fat: 0.0 g; Cholesterol: 0 mg; Sodium: 220 mg; Potassium: 190 mg; Total Carbohydrate: 14 g; Dietary Fiber: 6 g; Sugars: 2 g; Protein: 5 g; Phosphorus: 70 mg

Caponata-Style Sicilian Eggplant with Olives

SERVES: 16 **SERVING SIZE:** 1/4 cup eggplant mixture **HANDS-ON TIME:** 15 minutes
HANDS-OFF TIME: 22 minutes **TOTAL TIME:** 37 minutes (plus 8 hours chill time)

Caponata is basically a cooked sweet-and-sour vegetable salad and is mainly served as an appetizer, but it can also be served as a relish or topper for grilled fish, pork tenderloin, chicken, or turkey. Try it as a sandwich spread or a topper for quesadillas and turkey or meatless burgers. This recipe makes a lot, but you can do so much with it! This is definitely a crowd-pleasing kind of dish!

- 3/4 lb eggplant, cut into 1/2-inch cubes
- 1 cup chopped red bell pepper
- 3/4 cup chopped celery
- 1 (14.5-oz) can no-salt-added diced tomatoes
- 1/2 cup raisins
- 1 1/2 Tbsp dried basil
- 2 Tbsp balsamic vinegar
- 1/2 cup water
- 2 Tbsp tomato paste
- 4 oz slivered almonds, coarsely chopped
- 12 pitted kalamata olives, coarsely chopped
- 2 Tbsp extra-virgin olive oil
- 1/2 tsp salt

1 Combine the eggplant, bell pepper, celery, tomatoes, raisins, basil, vinegar, and water in the Instant Pot. Seal the lid, close the valve, and set the Manual/Pressure Cook button to 10 minutes.

2 Use a quick pressure release. When the valve drops, carefully remove the lid, stir in the tomato paste, almonds, olives, oil, and salt. Allow to cool to room temperature, then cover and refrigerate for at least 8 hours or overnight to allow flavors to absorb.

3 Serve at room temperature.

COOK'S NOTE
This dish can be served with pita bread or on fresh veggies, such as halved Roma tomatoes or cucumber slices, or Belgian endive leaves.

NUTRITION FACTS

Choices/Exchanges: 1/2 Carbohydrate, 1 Fat

Calories: 100; Calories from Fat: 50; Total Fat: 6.0 g; Saturated Fat: 0.6 g; Trans Fat: 0.0 g; Cholesterol: 0 mg; Sodium: 135 mg; Potassium: 240 mg; Total Carbohydrate: 9 g; Dietary Fiber: 2 g; Sugars: 5 g; Protein: 2 g; Phosphorus: 55 mg

Mushroom–Shallot Toasts

SERVES: 4 **SERVING SIZE:** About 6 Tbsp mushroom mixture and 3 slices bread (1 oz total)
HANDS-ON TIME: 15 minutes **HANDS-OFF TIME:** 11 minutes **TOTAL TIME:** 26 minutes

This appetizer has a sophisticated taste, but can be made without an elaborate amount of effort! Madeira wine or dry sherry can be found in inexpensive varieties, so you don't have to spend a lot for a powerful, flavorful ingredient—and it lasts for years!

- 1 cup water
- 12 oz sliced mushrooms
- 2 tsp canola oil
- 2 oz shallots, chopped
- 2 Tbsp Madeira wine or dry sherry
- 1/4 tsp dried thyme
- 2 Tbsp light butter with canola oil
- 2 Tbsp chopped fresh parsley
- 1/8 tsp salt
- 4 oz multigrain Italian loaf bread, cut into 12 slices and lightly toasted

1 Place the water and a steamer basket into the Instant Pot. Add the mushrooms to the steamer basket. Seal the lid, close the valve, and set the Manual/Pressure Cook button to 3 minutes.

2 Use a quick pressure release. When the valve drops, carefully remove the lid. Remove the mushrooms and steamer basket and discard the water.

3 Press the Cancel button and reset to Sauté. Then press the Adjust button to "More" or "High." Add the oil and tilt the pot to lightly coat the bottom. Add the shallots and cook for 2 minutes, or until golden on the edges. Add the mushrooms, wine, and thyme; cook for 2 minutes, or until most of the liquid has evaporated.

4 Turn off the heat and stir in the butter, parsley, and salt. Serve the mushrooms, on the toast slices, immediately for peak flavors.

NUTRITION FACTS

Choices/Exchanges: 1 Starch, 1 Nonstarchy Vegetable, 1 Fat

Calories: 150; Calories from Fat: 60; Total Fat: 7.0 g; Saturated Fat: 1.5 g; Trans Fat: 0.0 g; Cholesterol: 5 mg; Sodium: 240 mg; Potassium: 400 mg; Total Carbohydrate: 17 g; Dietary Fiber: 3 g; Sugars: 4 g; Protein: 7 g; Phosphorus: 150 mg

Brussels Sprouts with Sour Cream Dipping Sauce

SERVES: 4　**SERVING SIZE:** 6 Brussels sprouts and 2 Tbsp sauce　**HANDS-ON TIME:** 5 minutes
HANDS-OFF TIME: 7 minutes　**TOTAL TIME:** 12 minutes (plus 5 minutes standing time)

These Brussels sprouts are perfectly bite-size and are a welcome addition that goes beyond the typical "veggie tray" options. It's easy to keep track of your portions, too!

1	cup water
24	fresh Brussels sprouts, trimmed (about 1 lb total)
1	Tbsp extra-virgin olive oil
1/4	tsp salt
1/2	cup light sour cream
1	Tbsp prepared horseradish
1/2	tsp Dijon mustard

1　Place the water and a steamer basket in the Instant Pot. Add the Brussels sprouts to the steamer basket. Seal the lid, close the valve, and set the Manual/Pressure Cook button to 2 minutes.

2　Use a quick pressure release. When the valve drops, carefully remove the lid. Place the Brussels sprouts on a dinner plate, drizzle with the oil, and sprinkle with salt. Do not stir. Let stand for 5 minutes to absorb the flavors and cool slightly.

3　Combine the sour cream, horseradish, and mustard in a small bowl.

4　Serve the Brussels sprouts warm or at room temperature with wooden toothpicks or forks. Serve the sauce alongside for dipping.

NUTRITION FACTS

Choices/Exchanges: 2 Nonstarchy Vegetable, 1 1/2 Fat

Calories: 120; Calories from Fat: 50; Total Fat: 6.0 g; Saturated Fat: 2.5 g; Trans Fat: 0.0 g; Cholesterol: 10 mg; Sodium: 230 mg; Potassium: 490 mg; Total Carbohydrate: 13 g; Dietary Fiber: 4 g; Sugars: 5 g; Protein: 6 g; Phosphorus: 110 mg

Panko-Crusted Cauliflower Bites

SERVES: 4   **SERVING SIZE:** About 1 cup (6 florets) and 3 Tbsp crumb mixture   **HANDS-ON TIME:** 11 minutes
HANDS-OFF TIME: 6 minutes   **TOTAL TIME:** 17 minutes

This is really fast (and really good, especially *fast*) recipe. Have everything ready and measured out before you start to cook.

1/2 cup panko bread crumbs
  2 Tbsp grated Parmesan cheese
  1 Tbsp grated lemon zest
1/4 tsp salt
  1 cup water
 24 fresh cauliflower florets, about 1–1 1/2-inch pieces (1 lb total)
  2 Tbsp extra-virgin olive oil

1 Press the Sauté button, then press the Adjust button to "More" or "High." When the display says "Hot," add the bread crumbs and cook for 3 minutes, or until golden, stirring frequently. Place the bread crumbs in a small bowl and toss with the cheese, lemon zest, and salt. Set aside.

2 Place the water and a steamer basket in the Instant Pot. Add the cauliflower to the steamer basket. Seal the lid, close the valve, press the Cancel button, and set the Manual/Pressure Cook button to 1 minute.

3 Use a quick pressure release. When the valve drops, carefully remove the lid. Place the cauliflower on a dinner plate in a single layer, drizzle evenly with the oil, and sprinkle with the bread crumb mixture. Serve immediately, with wooden toothpicks or forks, for peak flavors and texture.

NUTRITION FACTS

Choices/Exchanges: 1/2 Starch, 1 Nonstarchy Vegetable, 1 1/2 Fat

Calories: 130; Calories from Fat: 60; Total Fat: 7.0 g; Saturated Fat: 1.3 g; Trans Fat: 0.0 g; Cholesterol: 0 mg; Sodium: 210 mg; Potassium: 360 mg; Total Carbohydrate: 13 g; Dietary Fiber: 3 g; Sugars: 3 g; Protein: 4 g; Phosphorus: 75 mg

Street Tacos with Beef

SERVES: 8   **SERVING SIZE:** 1/4 cup beef mixture, 2 Tbsp toppings. and 3 tortillas
HANDS-ON TIME: 23 minutes   **HANDS-OFF TIME:** 1 hour   **TOTAL TIME:** 1 hour and 23 minutes

This is a very popular "street food" in Mexico. You can find it everywhere you go! It's a great party food, too!

1 Tbsp canola oil
1 lb trimmed top round steak, cut into 4 pieces*
12 oz beer
1/4 cup lime juice
3/4 cup chopped fresh cilantro, divided
2 tsp smoked paprika
1 tsp garlic powder
2 tsp grated orange zest
1 Tbsp hot sauce (such as Frank's RedHot)
1 tsp ground cumin
1/2 tsp salt
1/4 tsp black pepper
24 "street taco" corn tortillas (such as Mission Street Taco Tortillas), warmed
1/2 cup finely chopped red onion

1 Press the Sauté button, then press the Adjust button to "More" or "High." When the display says "Hot," add the oil and tilt the Instant Pot to lightly coat the bottom. Add half of the beef and cook for 3 minutes on each side. Set aside and repeat with the remaining beef. Return the beef to the Instant Pot and add the beer, lime juice, 1/4 cup of the cilantro, smoked paprika, garlic powder, and orange zest.

2 Seal the lid, close the valve, press the Cancel button, and set the Manual/Pressure Cook button to 45 minutes.

3 Use a quick pressure release. When the valve drops, carefully remove the lid. Remove the beef with a slotted spoon and place on a cutting board and shred.

*When purchasing beef or pork, always buy about 8 oz more than you need. You will lose some of the weight after the meat is trimmed of fat.

4 Press the Cancel button and reset to Sauté. Then press the Adjust button to "More" or "High." Bring the liquid to boil and boil for 10 minutes, or until reduced to 1/2 cup of liquid. Turn off the heat and stir in the shredded beef, hot sauce, cumin, salt, and pepper.

5 Serve the beef mixture on tortillas and top with equal amounts of the remaining 1/2 cup of cilantro and the red onion.

NUTRITION FACTS

Choices/Exchanges: 1 1/2 Starch, 2 Lean Protein

Calories: 190; Calories from Fat: 45; Total Fat: 5.0 g; Saturated Fat: 0.9 g; Trans Fat: 0.0 g; Cholesterol: 30 mg; Sodium: 250 mg; Potassium: 270 mg; Total Carbohydrate: 24 g; Dietary Fiber: 3 g; Sugars: 3 g; Protein: 14 g; Phosphorus: 230 mg

Pickled Jalapeño Bean Bites

SERVES: 8   **SERVING SIZE:** 1/4 cup   **HANDS-ON TIME:** 5 minutes   **HANDS-OFF TIME:** 19 minutes
TOTAL TIME: 24 minutes (plus 2 hours chill time)

Super easy to make and so fun to serve—this is a great "nibble" food! Serve as is or alongside other low-carb items on a "cheese and veggie" board!

3/4 cup dried large lima beans or butter beans, rinsed and drained
3 cups water
1/4 cup pickled jalapeño slices (such as La Costeña Nachos pickled jalapeño peppers)
3 Tbsp extra-virgin olive oil
1 Tbsp cider vinegar
1 garlic clove, minced
1/2 tsp salt

1 Place the beans and water in the Instant Pot. Seal the lid, close the valve, and set the Manual/Pressure Cook button to 12 minutes.

2 Use a quick pressure release. Meanwhile, combine the remaining ingredients in a shallow dish, such as a glass pie pan. Set aside.

3 When the valve drops, carefully remove the lid. Drain the beans in a colander. Run under cold water for about 1 minute to stop the cooking process. Drain well.

4 Add the beans to the jalapeño mixture. Gently stir until well combined. Cover and refrigerate for at least 2 hours. You may want to stir occasionally.

5 Serve cold or at room temperature with wooden toothpicks.

COOK'S NOTE
Store leftovers in an airtight container in the refrigerator. Stir before serving.

NUTRITION FACTS
Choices/Exchanges: 1 Starch, 1/2 Fat
Calories: 100; Calories from Fat: 45; Total Fat: 5.0 g; Saturated Fat: 0.7 g; Trans Fat: 0.0 g; Cholesterol: 0 mg; Sodium: 250 mg; Potassium: 300 mg; Total Carbohydrate: 11 g; Dietary Fiber: 3 g; Sugars: 2 g; Protein: 4 g; Phosphorus: 65 mg

Herbed Quinoa-Stuffed Tomatoes

SERVES: 8   **SERVING SIZE:** 1/4 cup quinoa mixture and 3 tomato halves   **HANDS-ON TIME:** 15 minutes
HANDS-OFF TIME: 7 minutes   **TOTAL TIME:** 22 minutes

They're pretty, they're fun to eat, and they pop with flavor! The added bonus: these stuffed tomatoes are an excellent source of fiber and vitamin C.

2	Tbsp extra-virgin olive oil, divided
1	oz pine nuts or slivered almonds, coarsely chopped
1/2	cup dry organic quinoa (such as Bob's Red Mill)
2	cups water
3	Tbsp capers, chopped
1	Tbsp cider vinegar
1	small garlic clove, minced
2	tsp dried basil
1/2	tsp salt
1/8	tsp crushed pepper flakes
12	plum tomatoes, halved lengthwise and hollowed out

1 Press the Sauté button, then press the Adjust button to "More" or "High." When the display says "Hot," add 1 tsp of the oil to the Instant Pot, tilt the pot to lightly coat the bottom, and add the nuts. Cook for 2 minutes, stirring occasionally, then set aside in a medium bowl.

2 Place the quinoa, water, and 1 tsp of the oil in the pot. Seal the lid and close the valve. Press the Cancel button and reset to Manual/Pressure Cook for 2 minutes.

3 Use a quick pressure release. When the valve drops, carefully remove the lid. Drain the quinoa in a fine mesh sieve. Run under cold water; drain well.

4 Place the quinoa in the bowl with the nuts. Stir in the capers, vinegar, garlic, basil, salt, pepper flakes, and remaining oil.

5 Spoon equal amounts of the quinoa mixture into each of the tomato halves.

COOK'S NOTE

To "hollow out" the tomato halves easily, use a small teaspoon to scoop out the pulp and seeds.

NUTRITION FACTS

Choices/Exchanges: 1/2 Starch, 1 Nonstarchy Vegetable, 1 Fat

Calories: 120; Calories from Fat: 50; Total Fat: 6.0 g; Saturated Fat: 0.7 g; Trans Fat: 0.0 g; Cholesterol: 0 mg; Sodium: 230 mg; Potassium: 390 mg; Total Carbohydrate: 13 g; Dietary Fiber: 3 g; Sugars: 4 g; Protein: 3 g; Phosphorus: 100 mg

Stuffed Petite Peppers

SERVES: 4   **SERVING SIZE:** 3 stuffed peppers   **HANDS-ON TIME:** 14 minutes   **HANDS-OFF TIME:** 41 minutes
TOTAL TIME: 55 minutes (plus 5 minutes standing time)

This cooking technique prevents the peppers from losing their body and keeps the tender crunch of the nuts while creating an overall concentrated sweetness to the peppers.

12 petite sweet peppers (about 9 oz total)
1 cup water
1 1/2 oz crumbled reduced-fat blue cheese
1 1/2 oz pine nuts or slivered almonds, coarsely chopped
1 1/2 Tbsp dry organic quinoa (such as Bob's Red Mill)
6 Tbsp finely chopped red onion, divided
1 Tbsp plus 1 tsp extra-virgin olive oil, divided
1 tsp dried oregano
1 tsp hot sauce (such as Frank's RedHot)
1 (18-inch-long) sheet aluminum foil
3 cups arugula
1/4 tsp coarsely ground black pepper

1 Cut the tops off each pepper, leaving the whole pepper intact, and carefully scoop out the seeds using a small measuring spoon.

2 Place the water and a trivet in the Instant Pot.

3 In a medium bowl, combine the cheese, nuts, quinoa, 2 Tbsp of the red onion, 1 Tbsp of the oil, oregano, and hot sauce. Stuff each pepper cavity with cheese mixture, pressing down to pack slightly. Place the peppers in a 7-inch nonstick springform pan. Cover the pan entirely with foil.

4 Make a foil sling by folding an 18-inch-long piece of foil in half lengthwise. Place the pan in the center of the sling and lower the pan into the pot. Fold down the excess foil from the sling to allow the lid to close properly.

5 Seal the lid, close the valve, and set the Manual/Pressure Cook button to 25 minutes.

6   Use a natural pressure release for 10 minutes, followed by a quick pressure release. When the valve drops, carefully remove the lid. Remove the pan using the sling. Blot off any excess moisture that is on the foil before removing the foil. Remove the foil and let stand for 5 minutes to allow peppers and mixture to firm up slightly.

7   In a large bowl, combine the arugula, remaining 1 tsp of the oil, remaining 4 Tbsp of the red onion, and the black pepper. Toss to coat the arugula. Serve the peppers, warm or at room temperature, over a bed of the dressed arugula.

NUTRITION FACTS

Choices/Exchanges: 1/2 Carbohydrate, 1 Nonstarchy Vegetable, 2 1/2 Fat

Calories: 190; Calories from Fat: 130; Total Fat: 14.0 g; Saturated Fat: 2.5 g; Trans Fat: 0.0 g; Cholesterol: 5 mg; Sodium: 200 mg; Potassium: 330 mg; Total Carbohydrate: 11 g; Dietary Fiber: 3 g; Sugars: 4 g; Protein: 6 g; Phosphorus: 150 mg

Combo Main Dishes

6

Chicken Sausage and Zucchini–Stuffed Potatoes
page 106

Ginger, Lime, and Edamame Spaghetti Squash

page 118

Sausage and White Bean–Stuffed Portobellos
page 112

Creamy Chicken Pasta with Broccoli

SERVES: 4   **SERVING SIZE:** 1 1/2 cups   **HANDS-ON TIME:** 10 minutes   **HANDS-OFF TIME:** 15 minutes
TOTAL TIME: 25 minutes (plus 5 minutes standing time)

Oranges are not the only heroes that deliver vitamin C—this comforting, creamy pasta dish contains 90% of your vitamin C for the day!

- 1 lb boneless, skinless chicken breasts, cut into 1-inch pieces
- 4 oz uncooked multigrain rotini pasta (such as Barilla Protein Plus)
- 2 cups water
- 1/2 cup chopped sun-dried tomatoes (not oil-packed)
- 1 1/2 tsp dried oregano
- 3 cups fresh broccoli florets
- 4 oz reduced-fat garlic and herb soft cheese (such as Alouette)
- 1/4 tsp plus 1/8 tsp salt, divided
- 1/2 cup finely chopped green onion (both green and white parts)

1 Combine the chicken, pasta, water, tomatoes, and oregano in the Instant Pot. Stir, making sure the pasta is covered in water. Seal the lid, close the valve, and set the Manual/Pressure Cook button to 3 minutes.

2 Use a quick pressure release. When the valve drops, carefully remove the lid. Stir in the broccoli.

3 Seal the lid and close the valve. Press the Cancel button and reset to Manual/Pressure Cook for "0" minutes. When the front panel shows "0," use a quick pressure release. When the valve drops, carefully remove the lid.

4 Using a tablespoon, gradually add the cheese and stir very gently until melted. Add the green onion and 1/4 tsp of the salt. Turn off the heat. Let stand, uncovered, for 5 minutes to allow pasta to thicken slightly and absorb the flavors. Sprinkle with the remaining 1/8 tsp of salt.

NUTRITION FACTS

Choices/Exchanges: 1 Starch, 2 Nonstarchy Vegetable, 4 Lean Protein, 1/2 Fat

Calories: 320; Calories from Fat: 90; Total Fat: 10.0 g; Saturated Fat: 4.2 g; Trans Fat: 0.0 g; Cholesterol: 85 mg; Sodium: 480 mg; Potassium: 770 mg; Total Carbohydrate: 28 g; Dietary Fiber: 5 g; Sugars: 6 g; Protein: 33 g; Phosphorus: 345 mg

Lemon–Rosemary Chicken with Root Vegetables

SERVES: 4 **SERVING SIZE:** 1/4 of the chicken and about 1 1/4 cups vegetables **HANDS-ON TIME:** 15 minutes
HANDS-OFF TIME: 40 minutes **TOTAL TIME:** 55 minutes (plus 15 minutes standing time)

A good combo main dish doesn't have to be heavy on the carbs, but it should have a lot character, a variety of flavors, and good nutritional benefits. This dish pops with lemon while providing 200% of your daily requirement of vitamin A all in one pot!

- 8 oz carrots, cut into 2-inch pieces
- 8 oz parsnips, cut into 2-inch pieces
- 1 fennel bulb, top removed and cut into 8 wedges
- 1 cup dry white wine or water
- 1 tsp paprika
- 1 tsp dried rosemary
- 1 tsp garlic powder
- 1 large lemon, cut into 6 wedges, divided
- 1 (4-lb) whole fryer chicken
- 1 Tbsp canola oil
- 1/2 tsp salt, divided
- 1/2 tsp black pepper, divided

1 Place the carrots, parsnips, fennel, and wine in the Instant Pot. Combine the paprika, rosemary, and garlic powder in a small bowl.

2 Place 2 lemon wedges in the cavity of the chicken. Rub the oil evenly over the chicken and sprinkle with the paprika mixture. Place the chicken on top of the vegetables in the pot. Top with the remaining lemon wedges.

3 Seal the lid and close the valve. Set the Manual/Pressure Cook button to 27 minutes. Use a quick pressure release.

4 When the valve drops, carefully remove the lid. Carefully remove the chicken using 2 large spoons or a spoon and fork, and let stand for 15 minutes before slicing. Discard the skin.

5 Meanwhile, remove the vegetables with a slotted spoon, discarding the lemon, and place on a serving platter. Sprinkle the vegetables with 1/4 tsp of the salt and pepper. Cover to keep warm.

6 Once the chicken has been sliced, sprinkle the chicken evenly with the remaining 1/4 tsp of salt and pepper.

NUTRITION FACTS

Choices/Exchanges: 1/2 Starch, 2 Nonstarchy Vegetable, 6 Lean Protein, 1 1/2 Fat

Calories: 430; Calories from Fat: 160; Total Fat: 18.0 g; Saturated Fat: 4.4 g; Trans Fat: 0.0 g; Cholesterol: 115 mg; Sodium: 470 mg; Potassium: 940 mg; Total Carbohydrate: 21 g; Dietary Fiber: 6 g; Sugars: 7 g; Protein: 44 g; Phosphorus: 375 mg

Chicken Sausage and Zucchini–Stuffed Potatoes

SERVES: 4   **SERVING SIZE:** 8 oz potato and about 1/2 cup sausage mixture   **HANDS-ON TIME:** 18 minutes
HANDS-OFF TIME: 34 minutes   **TOTAL TIME:** 52 minutes

Hot baked potatoes topped with browned Italian sausage, Italian veggies, and blue cheese—all prepared in one pot! Grab a fork and enjoy!

- 2 Tbsp extra-virgin olive oil, divided
- 2 (3-oz) fully cooked Italian chicken sausage links (such as Al Fresco Asiago with Red Peppers), chopped
- 2 cups water, divided
- 1 medium zucchini, chopped
- 1 cup chopped green onion (both green and white parts), divided
- 1/2 tsp dried oregano
- 1 tsp hot sauce (such as Frank's RedHot)
- 4 russet potatoes (8 oz each), pierced in several areas with a fork
- 1/8 tsp salt
- 1/4 tsp black pepper
- 1 oz crumbled reduced-fat blue cheese

1. Press the Sauté button, then press the Adjust button to "More" or "High." When the display says "Hot," add 1 Tbsp of the oil and tilt the pot to lightly coat the bottom. Add the sausage and cook for 3 minutes, or until beginning to brown on the edges.

2. Add 1/3 cup of the water, the zucchini, 3/4 cup of the green onion, and the oregano. Cook for 3 minutes, or until zucchini is tender-crisp, scraping up the browned bits on the bottom of the pan as it's cooking.

3. Remove the sausage and zucchini to a medium bowl and combine with the hot sauce and remaining 1 Tbsp of oil. Cover to keep warm.

4 Put a steamer basket in the Instant Pot and add the remaining water. Add the potatoes to the steamer basket. Seal the lid and close the valve. Press the Cancel button and reset to Manual/Pressure Cook for 18 minutes.

5 Use a natural pressure release for 10 minutes, followed by a quick pressure release. When the valve drops, carefully remove the lid. Remove the potatoes with tongs (or a fork).

6 Split the potatoes almost in half and fluff with a fork. Add the salt and pepper to the sausage mixture and spoon equal amounts over each potato. Top with the cheese and remaining 1/4 cup of green onion.

NUTRITION FACTS

Choices/Exchanges: 2 1/2 Starch, 1 Nonstarchy Vegetable, 1 Lean Protein, 2 Fat

Calories: 350; Calories from Fat: 110; Total Fat: 12.0 g; Saturated Fat: 3.1 g;
Trans Fat: 0.0 g; Cholesterol: 40 mg; Sodium: 470 mg; Potassium: 1580 mg;
Total Carbohydrate: 45 g; Dietary Fiber: 6 g; Sugars: 6 g; Protein: 16 g;
Phosphorus: 250 mg

Turkey and Quinoa–Stuffed Peppers

SERVES: 4   **SERVING SIZE:** 1 stuffed pepper   **HANDS-ON TIME:** 15 minutes   **HANDS-OFF TIME:** 35 minutes
TOTAL TIME: 50 minutes

Red peppers, green chilies, and black beans—this colorful dish is definitely not your ordinary stuffed pepper!

- 4 large red bell peppers
- 8 oz 93% lean ground turkey
- 1/2 (15-oz) can no-salt-added black beans, rinsed and drained
- 1/3 cup dry organic quinoa (such as Bob's Red Mill)
- 1/2 cup chopped fresh cilantro, divided
- 1 egg
- 2 tsp smoked paprika
- 1/8 tsp cayenne pepper
- 1/4 tsp salt
- 2 (4-oz) cans chopped mild green chilies
- 1 cup water
- 1/4 cup light sour cream

1. Cut off the top portion of each pepper and chop the top portion only. Discard the seeds from the peppers.

2. Combine the turkey, the chopped portion of the peppers, the beans, quinoa, 1/4 cup cilantro, egg, paprika, cayenne pepper, salt, and all but 1/4 cup of the green chilies in a medium bowl. Stuff the peppers with the turkey mixture.

3. Place the water and a trivet in the Instant Pot and arrange the peppers on the trivet. Top each pepper with 1 Tbsp of the remaining green chilies.

4. Seal the lid, close the valve, and set the Manual/Pressure Cook button to 18 minutes.

5. Use a natural pressure release for about 12 minutes. When the valve drops, carefully remove the lid. Remove the peppers and top with equal amounts of sour cream and the remaining cilantro.

NUTRITION FACTS

Choices/Exchanges: 1 Starch, 3 Nonstarchy Vegetable, 2 Lean Protein, 1 Fat
Calories: 300; Calories from Fat: 80; Total Fat: 9.0 g; Saturated Fat: 2.8 g;
Trans Fat: 0.1 g; Cholesterol: 95 mg; Sodium: 450 mg; Potassium: 890 mg;
Total Carbohydrate: 34 g; Dietary Fiber: 8 g; Sugars: 13 g; Protein: 20 g;
Phosphorus: 325 mg

Spiced Lentils with Tomatoes and Cilantro

SERVES: 4   **SERVING SIZE:** About 1 cup   **HANDS-ON TIME:** 20 minutes   **HANDS-OFF TIME:** 15 minutes
TOTAL TIME: 35 minutes

Don't have time to do much prep work? Use 2 cups of frozen sliced carrots and 2 cups of pepper stir-fry veggies instead of the fresh carrots, onions, and peppers. The dish will take more time to come to pressure if you use frozen veggies, though.

- 4 oz dried brown or green lentils, rinsed and drained
- 2 cups sliced carrots
- 1 cup chopped onion
- 1 cup chopped red bell pepper
- 1 cup chopped tomato
- 2 cups water
- 1 tsp ground cumin
- 1/2 tsp ground turmeric
- 1 cup chopped fresh cilantro
- 2 Tbsp grated fresh ginger
- 3 Tbsp lime juice
- 1 1/2 tsp sugar
- 1/2 tsp salt
- 2 Tbsp extra-virgin olive oil
- 2 tsp hot sauce (such as Frank's RedHot)

1 Combine the lentils, carrots, onion, bell pepper, tomatoes, water, cumin, and turmeric in the Instant Pot. Seal the lid, close the valve, and set the Manual/Pressure Cook button to 8 minutes.

2 Use a quick pressure release. When the valve drops, carefully remove the lid.

3 Add the remaining ingredients to the Instant Pot. Press the Cancel button and set to Sauté. Then press the Adjust button to "More" or "High." Bring to a boil and boil for 5 minutes to thicken slightly, stirring frequently.

COOK'S NOTE

You can use more or less sugar and/or hot sauce in this recipe to suit your tastes. Just keep in mind that using more of these ingredients will add some calories and grams of carbohydrate to your meal.

NUTRITION FACTS

Choices/Exchanges: 1 Starch, 3 Nonstarchy Vegetable, 1 1/2 Fat

Calories: 230; Calories from Fat: 70; Total Fat: 8.0 g; Saturated Fat: 1.1 g;
Trans Fat: 0.0 g; Cholesterol: 0 mg; Sodium: 450 mg; Potassium: 800 mg;
Total Carbohydrate: 33 g; Dietary Fiber: 10 g; Sugars: 11 g; Protein: 9 g;
Phosphorus: 190 mg

Italian Herb Meatloaf and Zucchini Halves

SERVES: 4   **SERVING SIZE:** 1 slice meatloaf (1/4 loaf) and 2 squash halves   **HANDS-ON TIME:** 15 minutes
HANDS-OFF TIME: 50 minutes   **TOTAL TIME:** 1 hour and 5 minutes (plus 10 minutes standing time)

This recipe makes a great one-dish meal, or you can omit the zucchini, oil, and salt, and it can stand alone as a combo main dish!

- 2/3 cup reduced-sodium marinara sauce (such as Prego Heart Smart), divided
- 2 Tbsp ketchup
- 12 oz 93% lean ground turkey
- 4 oz sweet Italian turkey sausage (such as Foster Farms), removed from casing

- 1 cup chopped green bell pepper
- 1/3 cup dry organic quinoa (such as Bob's Red Mill)
- 1 egg
- 1 1/2 tsp dried Italian seasoning
- 1 tsp Worcestershire sauce
- 1 1/2 cups water

- 3 (18-inch-long) sheets aluminum foil Nonstick cooking spray
- 1 Tbsp extra-virgin olive oil
- 4 medium zucchini, halved lengthwise (or 2 zucchini and 2 crookneck squash)
- 1/8 tsp black pepper

1 Combine 2 Tbsp of the marinara sauce with the ketchup in a small bowl and set aside.

2 Combine the remaining marinara sauce with the turkey, sausage, bell pepper, quinoa, egg, Italian seasoning, and Worcestershire sauce in a medium bowl.

3 On a dinner plate, shape the turkey mixture into a loaf about 5 x 7 x 1 1/2 inches. Place the water and a trivet in the Instant Pot.

4 Fold each of the foil sheets in half lengthwise, and coat the foil strips with cooking spray. Crisscross the strips in a spoke-like fashion to act as a sling. Slide the loaf off of the plate and onto the center of the "spokes." Lift the ends

of the foil strips to place the loaf on the trivet. Tuck in the ends of the foil strips to close the lid easily. Seal the lid, close the valve, and set the Manual/Pressure Cook button to 35 minutes.

5 Use a quick pressure release. When the valve drops, carefully remove the lid. Remove the meatloaf and sling carefully using the ends of the foil, and place the foil and meatloaf on a cutting board. (Do not discard the water in the Instant Pot.) Spoon the reserved ketchup mixture evenly over the meatloaf and let stand for 10 minutes before slicing.

6 Meanwhile, drizzle the oil evenly over the cut sides of the zucchini, sprinkle with pepper, and place 4 zucchini halves on the trivet. Top with the remaining 4 halves. Seal the lid, close the valve, press the Cancel button, and reset to Manual/Pressure Cook for 3 minutes.

7 Use a quick pressure release. Serve the zucchini alongside the meatloaf.

NUTRITION FACTS

Choices/Exchanges: 1 Starch, 2 Nonstarchy Vegetable, 3 Lean Protein, 2 Fat
Calories: 350; Calories from Fat: 150; Total Fat: 17.0 g; Saturated Fat: 4.0 g;
Trans Fat: 0.2 g; Cholesterol: 125 mg; Sodium: 490 mg; Potassium: 1130 mg;
Total Carbohydrate: 25 g; Dietary Fiber: 5 g; Sugars: 11 g; Protein: 28 g;
Phosphorus: 405 mg

Sausage and White Bean–Stuffed Portobellos

SERVES: 4 **SERVING SIZE:** 1 stuffed mushroom (about 6 oz) **HANDS-ON TIME:** 17 minutes
HANDS-OFF TIME: 16 minutes **TOTAL TIME:** 33 minutes (plus 5 minutes standing time)

People say that we eat with our eyes—well, this is the perfect dish for it! It's absolutely beautiful and tastes scrumptious, too! Serve these portobellos at the kitchen counter or by candlelight. They're perfect either way.

Nonstick cooking spray
4 oz sweet Italian turkey sausage (such as Foster Farms), removed from casing
1/2 cup no-salt-added tomato sauce
1 Tbsp dried basil
1/4 tsp crushed pepper flakes
4 large portobello mushroom caps, wiped clean with a damp cloth (about 12 oz total)
1/2 (15-oz) can no-salt-added navy beans, rinsed and drained
3/4 cup chopped red bell pepper
1 cup water
2 oz fresh spinach, coarsely chopped
4 oz shredded part-skim mozzarella cheese
2 Tbsp grated Parmesan cheese

1 Press the Sauté button, then press the Adjust button to "More" or "High." When the display says "Hot," coat the Instant Pot with cooking spray. Add the sausage to the pot and cook for 2 minutes, or until it begins to brown on the edges, stirring frequently. Remove from the Instant Pot and set aside.

2 Combine the tomato sauce, basil, and pepper flakes in a small bowl. Spoon equal amounts of the sauce on top of each mushroom (gill side up). Top with equal amounts of the sausage, beans, and bell pepper.

3 Add the water to the Instant Pot and top with a steamer basket. Place the mushrooms in the steamer basket, overlapping slightly, if necessary. Seal the lid, close the valve, and set the Manual/Pressure Cook button to 10 minutes.

4 Use a quick pressure release. When the valve drops, carefully remove the lid. Top the mushrooms with the spinach and mozzarella. Cover, but do not seal the lid, and let stand for 5 minutes to allow the spinach to wilt slightly. Sprinkle with the Parmesan and serve.

NUTRITION FACTS

Choices/Exchanges: 1/2 Starch, 2 Nonstarchy Vegetable, 2 Lean Protein, 1 Fat

Calories: 210; Calories from Fat: 70; Total Fat: 8.0 g; Saturated Fat: 3.9 g; Trans Fat: 0.1 g; Cholesterol: 35 mg; Sodium: 400 mg; Potassium: 780 mg; Total Carbohydrate: 17 g; Dietary Fiber: 5 g; Sugars: 4 g; Protein: 18 g; Phosphorus: 355 mg

Wild and Brown Walnut Rice

SERVES: 4 **SERVING SIZE:** 1 1/4 cups **HANDS-ON TIME:** 12 minutes **HANDS-OFF TIME:** 25 minutes
TOTAL TIME: 37 minutes

This dish is an earthy combination of nutty brown and wild rice layered with rich flavors from the soy sauce, Sriracha-style hot sauce, cilantro and fresh lime, and a generous amount of walnuts.

2/3 cup wild rice
1/3 cup brown rice
3 cups water
3 Tbsp reduced-sodium soy sauce
2 Tbsp lime juice
2 tsp sesame oil
1 tsp Sriracha-style hot sauce
2 cups fresh or frozen sugar snap peas, thawed if frozen
3 oz chopped walnuts
1/2 cup chopped fresh cilantro or fresh basil (or 1/4 cup of each)
1/2 cup chopped green onion (both green and white parts)
1 lime, cut into 4 wedges

1 Combine the wild rice and brown rice in a fine mesh sieve and rinse under cold running water; drain well. Place the drained rice and the water in the Instant Pot.

2 Seal the lid, close the valve, and set the Manual/Pressure Cook button to 20 minutes.

3 Use a quick pressure release. Meanwhile, combine the soy sauce, lime juice, oil, and Sriracha-style hot sauce in a small bowl and set aside.

4 When the valve drops, carefully remove the lid. Stir in the sugar snap peas. Close the lid, but do not seal, and let stand for 1 minute to heat through. Drain well in a colander and shake off the excess liquid.

5 Place the rice mixture in a shallow serving bowl or a 1 1/2- or 2-quart casserole dish. Top with the walnuts, soy sauce mixture, cilantro, and green onion. Serve with the lime wedges to squeeze over all.

NUTRITION FACTS

Choices/Exchanges: 2 1/2 Starch, 1 Nonstarchy Vegetable, 3 Fat

Calories: 350; Calories from Fat: 150; Total Fat: 17.0 g; Saturated Fat: 1.8 g; Trans Fat: 0.0 g; Cholesterol: 0 mg; Sodium: 450 mg; Potassium: 730 mg; Total Carbohydrate: 42 g; Dietary Fiber: 5 g; Sugars: 4 g; Protein: 10 g; Phosphorus: 280 mg

Shrimp and Artichoke Pasta

SERVES: 4 **SERVING SIZE:** 1 1/2 cups **HANDS-ON TIME:** 7 minutes **HANDS-OFF TIME:** 17 minutes
TOTAL TIME: 24 minutes

It doesn't get much faster than this! Just cook, toss, and serve! Start to finish in less than 25 minutes.

- 4 oz uncooked multigrain rotini pasta (such as Barilla Protein Plus)
- 1 (9-oz) package frozen artichoke hearts
- 4 cups water
- 3 Tbsp extra-virgin olive oil, divided
- 2 cups packed baby spinach (2 oz)
- 1/2 cup chopped red onion
- 2 Tbsp cider vinegar
- 1 Tbsp dried oregano
- 1 garlic clove, minced
- 1/2 tsp salt
- 12 oz peeled raw shrimp*

1 Combine the rotini, frozen artichokes, water, and 1 Tbsp of the oil in the Instant Pot.

2 Seal the lid, close the valve, and set the Manual/Pressure Cook button to 3 minutes.

3 Use a quick pressure release. Meanwhile, combine the spinach, onion, vinegar, oregano, garlic, salt, and remaining 2 Tbsp of oil in a large bowl. Set aside.

4 When the valve drops, carefully remove the lid. Add the shrimp.

*If possible, use fresh (never frozen) shrimp or shrimp that are free of preservatives (for example, shrimp that have not been treated with salt or STPP [sodium tripolyphosphate]).

5 Seal the lid, close the valve, press the Cancel button, and reset to Manual/Pressure Cook for 1 minute.

6 Use a quick pressure release. Drain well, shaking off the excess liquid. Place the pasta in the bowl with the remaining ingredients and toss (using two utensils) until well blended and the spinach is slightly wilted.

NUTRITION FACTS

Choices/Exchanges: 1 Starch, 2 Nonstarchy Vegetable, 3 Lean Protein, 1 Fat

Calories: 300; Calories from Fat: 90; Total Fat: 10.0 g; Saturated Fat: 1.4 g; Trans Fat: 0.0 g; Cholesterol: 160 mg; Sodium: 450 mg; Potassium: 610 mg; Total Carbohydrate: 28 g; Dietary Fiber: 7 g; Sugars: 2 g; Protein: 28 g; Phosphorus: 335 mg

Ginger, Lime, and Edamame Spaghetti Squash

SERVES: 6   **SERVING SIZE:** About 1 1/2 cups   **HANDS-ON TIME:** 20 minutes   **HANDS-OFF TIME:** 17 minutes
TOTAL TIME: 37 minutes

Are you new to spaghetti squash? There are a few things to know: how to cut it in half, not to cook it too long, and how to get nice long strands. This recipe will teach you. It's all about the technique and the timing! Because of its light texture, spaghetti squash works particularly well in Asian dishes.

1 (3-lb) spaghetti squash
1 cup water
3 Tbsp reduced-sodium soy sauce
2 limes, divided
4 tsp sugar
1 Tbsp grated fresh ginger
1/8 tsp crushed pepper flakes
12 oz frozen shelled edamame
1 cup matchstick carrots
1/2 cup green onion (both green and white parts)
2 oz unsalted peanuts or slivered almonds, coarsely chopped
1/2 cup chopped fresh cilantro

1 Pierce the squash over the entire surface with the tip of a sharp knife. Place in the microwave and set on high for 2 minutes. Using 2 dish towels or pot holders, carefully remove the squash from the microwave (it will be hot). Cut the squash in half crosswise, not lengthwise. Scrape out the seeds and connecting strands with a spoon.

2 Place the water and a trivet in the Instant Pot. Place the 2 squash halves on the trivet. Seal the lid, close the valve, and set the Manual/Pressure Cook button to 7 minutes.

3 Use a quick pressure release. Meanwhile, combine the soy sauce, juice of 1 of the limes, sugar, ginger, and pepper flakes in a small bowl. Whisk until well blended and set aside.

4 When the valve drops, carefully remove the lid. Remove the squash halves and place on a cutting board. Remove the trivet.

5   Press the Cancel button and set to Sauté. Then press the Adjust button to "More" or "High." Add the edamame to the water, bring to a boil, and boil for 2 minutes. Drain well.

6   To create long spaghetti squash strands, run a fork around the outer edges of the squash to release the strands, rather than "raking through" the strands.

7   Place the squash in a large serving bowl or divide among 6 individual bowls. Top the squash evenly with the edamame, carrots, and green onion, spoon the soy sauce mixture evenly over all, and sprinkle with the nuts and cilantro. Do not stir. Cut the remaining lime into 6 wedges and serve with the squash to squeeze over all.

NUTRITION FACTS

Choices/Exchanges: 1/2 Starch, 2 Nonstarchy Vegetable, 1 Lean Protein, 1 Fat
Calories: 180; Calories from Fat: 70; Total Fat: 8.0 g; Saturated Fat: 0.7 g;
Trans Fat: 0.0 g; Cholesterol: 0 mg; Sodium: 320 mg; Potassium: 820 mg;
Total Carbohydrate: 21 g; Dietary Fiber: 6 g; Sugars: 9 g; Protein: 10 g;
Phosphorus: 160 mg

Easy Cheesy Beef, Veggie, and Rotini Casserole

SERVES: 4   **SERVING SIZE:** About 1 1/4 cups   **HANDS-ON TIME:** 14 minutes   **HANDS-OFF TIME:** 11 minutes
TOTAL TIME: 25 minutes

This "casserole-in-a-pot" is a great standby when you're running late. Beef, cheese, and pasta—yes!

Nonstick cooking spray
8 oz extra-lean (95% lean) ground beef
3 cups water
2 cups frozen mixed vegetables (such as Birdseye)
4 oz uncooked multigrain rotini pasta (such as Barilla Protein Plus)
1 Tbsp canola oil
1 1/4 cups chopped green onion (both green and white parts), divided
1/4 tsp black pepper
1/8 tsp cayenne pepper
4 oz shredded reduced-fat sharp cheddar cheese
1/4 tsp plus 1/8 tsp salt, divided

1 Press the Sauté button, then press the Adjust button to "More" or "High." When the display says "Hot," coat the Instant Pot with cooking spray. Add the beef and cook until browned, stirring occasionally. Remove and set aside.

2 Add the water, frozen vegetables, pasta, and oil to the Instant Pot, making sure the pasta is covered with water. Seal the lid, close the valve, press the Cancel button, and reset to Manual/Pressure Cook for 4 minutes.

3 Use a quick pressure release. When the valve drops, carefully remove the lid. Drain the pasta mixture, reserving 1/2 cup of the cooking liquid. Return the pasta mixture, the reserved 1/2 cup of liquid, 1 cup of the green onion, the black pepper, cayenne, and beef to the Instant Pot. Stir until well blended.

4 Add the cheese and 1/4 tsp of the salt; stir until the cheese is just melted. Top the pasta with the remaining 1/4 cup of green onion and sprinkle with the remaining salt.

NUTRITION FACTS

Choices/Exchanges: 1 1/2 Starch, 1 Nonstarchy Vegetable, 3 Lean Protein, 1 1/2 Fat

Calories: 350; Calories from Fat: 130; Total Fat: 14.0 g; Saturated Fat: 4.7 g;
Trans Fat: 0.1 g; Cholesterol: 55 mg; Sodium: 470 mg; Potassium: 510 mg;
Total Carbohydrate: 30 g; Dietary Fiber: 4 g; Sugars: 4 g; Protein: 26 g;
Phosphorus: 390 mg

So Simple Protein-Based Entrées

7

Panko-Crusted Cod
page 129

Super Quick Provolone Chicken Breasts

SERVES: 4   **SERVING SIZE:** About 4 oz cooked chicken and 1 slice provolone   **HANDS-ON TIME:** 7 minutes
HANDS-OFF TIME: 17 minutes   **TOTAL TIME:** 24 minutes (plus 5 minutes standing time)

This simple entrée is loaded with fresh *and* dried herbs and topped with *two* cheeses. Enough said!

- 4 (6-oz) boneless, skinless chicken breasts, trimmed of fat
- 1 tsp dried Italian seasoning
- 1 tsp onion powder
- 1/4 tsp crushed pepper flakes
- 1 cup water
- 1/4 tsp salt
- 1/8 tsp coarsely ground black pepper
- 1/4 cup chopped fresh basil
- 4 slices reduced-fat smoked provolone cheese (3/4 oz each)
- 4 tsp grated Parmesan cheese

1 Sprinkle the chicken breasts with Italian seasoning, onion powder, and pepper flakes.

2 Place the water and a steamer basket in the Instant Pot. Place the chicken breasts in the steamer basket, overlapping slightly. Seal the lid, close the valve, and set the Manual/Pressure Cook button to 5 minutes.

3 Use a natural pressure release for 5 minutes, followed by a quick pressure release. When the valve drops, carefully remove the lid. Remove the chicken and sprinkle evenly with the salt, pepper, and basil. Top with the cheese slices and Parmesan. Let stand for 5 minutes to allow cheese to melt slightly.

> **COOK'S NOTE**
> You can stick the chicken breasts under the broiler for 1 minute, if desired, to lightly brown. But watch closely so the cheese doesn't burn.

NUTRITION FACTS

Choices/Exchanges: 6 Lean Protein

Calories: 250; Calories from Fat: 70; Total Fat: 8.0 g; Saturated Fat: 3.7 g; Trans Fat: 0.0 g; Cholesterol: 110 mg; Sodium: 400 mg; Potassium: 350 mg; Total Carbohydrate: 2 g; Dietary Fiber: 0 g; Sugars: 0 g; Protein: 42 g; Phosphorus: 380 mg

Hurried Curried Chicken

SERVES: 6   **SERVING SIZE:** 1 chicken thigh and 1/3 cup sauce   **HANDS-ON TIME:** 15 minutes
HANDS-OFF TIME: 21 minutes   **TOTAL TIME:** 36 minutes

Sometimes it's nice to just grab a little something from the pantry to help with dinner. This is one of those times!

1 Tbsp canola oil
6 bone-in chicken thighs (about 2 lb total), skin removed
1/3 cup water
Juice of 1 lime
1 (15-oz) jar butter chicken simmer sauce (such as Patak's)
1/4 cup plain nonfat Greek yogurt
1 Tbsp grated fresh ginger
1/4 tsp salt
1/2 cup chopped green onion or fresh cilantro

1 Press the Sauté button, then press the Adjust button to "More" or "High." When the display says "Hot," add the oil and tilt the pot to lightly coat the bottom. Add the chicken, smooth side down, and cook for 5 minutes. Turn the chicken pieces over and top with the water and lime juice. Pour the butter chicken sauce over all, and do NOT stir. Seal the lid, close the valve, and set the Manual/Pressure Cook button to 15 minutes.

2   Use a quick pressure release. When the valve drops, carefully remove the lid. Turn off the heat and remove the chicken. Place the chicken in a shallow serving bowl and set aside. Remove 1/4 cup of the sauce from the pot and place it in a small bowl; whisk in the yogurt, ginger, and salt. Stir the yogurt mixture into the pot. Stir until well blended, pour the sauce over the chicken pieces, and sprinkle with the green onion.

NUTRITION FACTS

Choices/Exchanges: 1/2 Carbohydrate, 3 Lean Protein, 1 1/2 Fat

Calories: 230; Calories from Fat: 120; Total Fat: 13.0 g; Saturated Fat: 3.4 g; Trans Fat: 0.0 g; Cholesterol: 110 mg; Sodium: 370 mg; Potassium: 370 mg; Total Carbohydrate: 10 g; Dietary Fiber: 1 g; Sugars: 6 g; Protein: 20 g; Phosphorus: 250 mg

Jalapeño–Avocado Salmon

SERVES: 4   **SERVING SIZE:** 3 oz cooked salmon and about 2/3 cup avocado mixture
HANDS-ON TIME: 8 minutes   **HANDS-OFF TIME:** 10 minutes   **TOTAL TIME:** 18 minutes

We all know that salmon is so good for us, and if it's easy to make and tastes great it will be served more often, right? Keep it simple with this recipe!

4 (4-oz) salmon fillets (each about 3/4 inch thick)*
1/2 tsp dried oregano
1/8 tsp paprika
1/2 tsp salt, divided
1 cup water
2 avocados, peeled and chopped
1 cup chopped cucumber
1 jalapeño, seeded (if desired) and finely chopped
1/4 cup chopped fresh cilantro
1 lime, halved, divided

1 Sprinkle the salmon with the oregano, paprika, and 1/4 tsp of the salt.

2 Place the water and a steamer basket in the Instant Pot. Add the salmon to the steamer basket. Seal the lid, close the valve, and set the Manual/Pressure Cook button to 3 minutes.

3 Use a quick pressure release. Meanwhile, combine the avocado, cucumber, jalapeño, cilantro, juice of 1/2 lime, and the remaining 1/4 tsp of salt in a medium bowl.

4 When the valve drops, carefully remove the lid. Remove the steamer basket and salmon from the pot.

5 Serve the salmon topped with the avocado mixture. Cut the remaining lime half into 4 wedges and serve with the salmon to squeeze over all.

*If the salmon is less than 3/4 inch thick, cook for 2 minutes instead of 3 minutes.

NUTRITION FACTS

Choices/Exchanges: 1/2 Fruit, 4 Lean Protein, 1 1/2 Fat

Calories: 280; Calories from Fat: 140; Total Fat: 16.0 g; Saturated Fat: 2.5 g; Trans Fat: 0.0 g; Cholesterol: 60 mg; Sodium: 390 mg; Potassium: 860 mg; Total Carbohydrate: 9 g; Dietary Fiber: 5 g; Sugars: 1 g; Protein: 27 g; Phosphorus: 340 mg

Italian Parmesan Chicken Thighs

SERVES: 4   **SERVING SIZE:** 1 chicken thigh and 1/4 cup sauce   **HANDS-ON TIME:** 11 minutes
HANDS-OFF TIME: 31 minutes   **TOTAL TIME:** 42 minutes

This classic dish is a kid favorite and picky-eater-pleaser. It's a winner all the way around! Chicken cooked with pizza sauce and topped with Parmesan—they'll love it!

COOK'S NOTE

You can serve this chicken over cooked multigrain pasta, such as Barilla Protein Plus, if desired. I suggest using 1/2 cup of cooked pasta per serving if it fits with your meal plan.

Many supermarkets sell bone-in chicken thighs without the skin, but if yours doesn't, use paper towels to remove the skin. Hold a piece of chicken with a paper towel and use another towel in the other hand to help you pull the skin off. The paper towel gives you "traction" so the skin doesn't slip around while you're trying to remove it.

4 bone-in chicken thighs (about 1 3/4 lb total), skin removed
1 cup pizza sauce
2 tsp balsamic vinegar
2 tsp dried oregano
1/4 tsp crushed pepper flakes
1/4 cup grated Parmesan cheese

1 Place the chicken thighs in the Instant Pot and top with the remaining ingredients, except the Parmesan. Do not stir.

2 Seal the lid, close the valve, and set the Manual/Pressure Cook button to 15 minutes.

3 Use a natural pressure release for 10 minutes, followed by a quick pressure release.

4 When the valve drops, carefully remove the lid. Remove the chicken with a slotted spoon.

5 Press the Cancel button and set to Sauté. Then press the Adjust button to "More" or "High." Bring the sauce to a boil and boil for 7 minutes, or until reduced to 1 cup, stirring occasionally. Spoon the sauce evenly over the chicken pieces and top with the cheese.

NUTRITION FACTS

Choices/Exchanges: 1/2 Carbohydrate, 4 Lean Protein, 1/2 Fat

Calories: 220; Calories from Fat: 90; Total Fat: 10.0 g; Saturated Fat: 3.2 g; Trans Fat: 0.0 g; Cholesterol: 135 mg; Sodium: 400 mg; Potassium: 510 mg; Total Carbohydrate: 6 g; Dietary Fiber: 1 g; Sugars: 3 g; Protein: 26 g; Phosphorus: 280 mg

Turkey Breast and Chipotle Au Jus

SERVES: 12   **SERVING SIZE:** 3 oz cooked turkey and about 2 Tbsp sauce   **HANDS-ON TIME:** 12 minutes
HANDS-OFF TIME: 48 minutes   **TOTAL TIME:** 1 hour (plus 15 minutes standing time)

Turkey breasts vary slightly in size, of course. A general rule of thumb is to cook for 6 minutes for every pound. In other words, a 5-lb turkey breast should cook for 30 minutes and a 6-lb turkey breast should cook for 36 minutes. Easy math for an easy entrée!

2 Tbsp extra-virgin olive oil
2 chipotle chile peppers (canned in adobo sauce), minced
2 tsp rubbed sage
2 tsp grated orange zest
1/2 tsp salt
1/2 tsp black pepper
1 (5 1/2-lb) bone-in turkey breast (thawed if frozen)
1 large onion, cut into wedges
1 1/4 cups water

1 Combine the oil, chipotle chilies, sage, orange zest, salt, and pepper in a small bowl. Brush evenly over the turkey.

2 Place the onions and water in the bottom of the Instant Pot. Top with the turkey breast (cavity side up). Seal the lid, close the valve, and set the Manual/Pressure Cook button to 33 minutes.

3 Use a natural pressure release for 10 minutes, followed by a quick pressure release. When the valve drops, carefully remove the lid. Remove the turkey and set aside on a cutting board. Let stand for 15 minutes and then remove the skin and slice.

4 Meanwhile, press the Cancel button and set to Sauté. Then press the Adjust button to "More" or "High." Bring the cooking liquid and onions to a boil and boil for 5 minutes, or until reduced to 1 1/2 cups of liquid. Serve with sliced turkey.

COOK'S NOTE

Use leftover turkey to fill tortilla wraps, stuff pitas or sandwiches, or in salads and soups. It's fun to use this turkey for lettuce wraps, too!

NUTRITION FACTS

Choices/Exchanges: 3 Lean Protein

Calories: 150; Calories from Fat: 35; Total Fat: 4.0 g; Saturated Fat: 0.8 g; Trans Fat: 0.0 g; Cholesterol: 70 mg; Sodium: 190 mg; Potassium: 250 mg; Total Carbohydrate: 2 g; Dietary Fiber: 0 g; Sugars: 1 g; Protein: 26 g; Phosphorus: 200 mg

Panko-Crusted Cod

SERVES: 4   **SERVING SIZE:** About 4 oz cooked fish and 2 Tbsp bread crumb mixture
HANDS-ON TIME: 10 minutes   **HANDS-OFF TIME:** 8 minutes   **TOTAL TIME:** 18 minutes

Crunchy and light Japanese bread crumbs tossed with olive oil and lemon zest and mounded on top of lemon-splashed tender fish fillets with a hint of thyme are only minutes away!

1/2 cup panko bread crumbs
2 Tbsp extra-virgin olive oil
2 tsp grated lemon zest
1/4 tsp salt
1/4 cup light mayonnaise
2 tsp lemon juice
1/2 tsp dried thyme
4 (6-oz) cod fillets (each about 3/4 inch thick)
1 cup water
1 lemon, cut into 4 wedges

1 Press the Sauté button, then press the Adjust button to "More" or "High." When the display says "Hot," add the bread crumbs and cook for 2 minutes, or until golden brown, stirring frequently. Stir in the oil, lemon zest, and salt. Remove from the pot and set aside on a plate.

2 In a small bowl, combine the mayonnaise, lemon juice, and thyme. Spread equal amounts over the top of each cod fillet.

3 Place the water and a steamer basket in the Instant Pot. Add the fish to the steamer basket, mayonnaise side up. Seal the lid, close the valve, press the Cancel button, and set to Manual/Pressure Cook for 3 minutes.

4 Use a quick pressure release. When the valve drops, carefully remove the lid. Remove the steamer basket and fish from the pot. Serve the fish topped with the bread crumb mixture. Serve with the lemon wedges to squeeze over all.

NUTRITION FACTS

Choices/Exchanges: 1/2 Starch, 4 Lean Protein, 1 Fat

Calories: 270; Calories from Fat: 100; Total Fat: 11.0 g; Saturated Fat: 1.2 g; Trans Fat: 0.0 g; Cholesterol: 75 mg; Sodium: 370 mg; Potassium: 740 mg; Total Carbohydrate: 10 g; Dietary Fiber: 1 g; Sugars: 2 g; Protein: 31 g; Phosphorus: 360 mg

Chipotle–Cumin Shredded Brisket

SERVES: 7   **SERVING SIZE:** 1/2 cup brisket   **HANDS-ON TIME:** 23 minutes
HANDS-OFF TIME: 1 hour and 20 minutes   **TOTAL TIME:** 1 hour and 43 minutes

This is definitely one of those "how-many-ways-can-it-be-served" recipes! Serve it as is or over warmed corn tortillas, with taco salad, in lettuce wraps, or over mashed sweet potatoes, veggie spirals, or brown rice. The list goes on and on—and it freezes well, too!

1 Tbsp canola oil
2 1/2 lb trimmed flat-cut beef brisket, cut into 3-inch pieces*
1 cup chopped onion
1 cup water
2 Tbsp lime juice
1 1/2 Tbsp ground cumin, divided
2 tsp ground chipotle pepper, divided
1 1/2 tsp garlic powder
1 tsp ground allspice
3 dried bay leaves
2 Tbsp tomato paste
3/4 tsp salt

1 Press the Sauté button, then press the Adjust button to "More" or "High." When the display says "Hot," add the oil and tilt the pot to lightly coat the bottom. Working in 2 batches, add half of the beef and cook for 3 minutes on each side. Remove and set aside. Repeat with the remaining beef.

2 Return the beef and any accumulated juices to the pot with the onions, water, and lime juice. Top with 1 Tbsp of the cumin, 1 tsp of the chipotle, the garlic powder, allspice, and bay leaves. Seal the lid, close the valve, press the Cancel button, and set to Manual/Pressure Cook for 75 minutes.

*When purchasing beef or pork, always buy about 8 oz more than you need. You will lose some of the weight after the meat is trimmed of fat.

3 Use a quick pressure release. When the valve drops, carefully remove the lid. Place a colander over a bowl and drain the beef mixture, reserving 1 cup of the cooking liquid. (Discard the remaining liquid and bay leaves.)

4 Return the drained beef mixture to the Instant Pot. Take the 1 cup of reserved liquid and stir in the tomato paste, salt, remaining 1 1/2 tsp cumin, and 1 tsp chipotle. Stir until well blended. Add to the beef mixture and stir until blended.

NUTRITION FACTS

Choices/Exchanges: 4 Lean Protein, 1 Fat

Calories: 240; Calories from Fat: 110; Total Fat: 12.0 g; Saturated Fat: 3.6 g; Trans Fat: 0.0 g; Cholesterol: 90 mg; Sodium: 320 mg; Potassium: 370 mg; Total Carbohydrate: 3 g; Dietary Fiber: 1 g; Sugars: 1 g; Protein: 29 g; Phosphorus: 240 mg

Chuck with Red Wine'd Mushrooms

SERVES: 5   **SERVING SIZE:** About 3/4 cup beef mixture   **HANDS-ON TIME:** 20 minutes
HANDS-OFF TIME: 1 hour and 15 minutes   **TOTAL TIME:** 1 hour and 35 minutes

Beef cooked with red wine is always a guaranteed hit, but you can branch out and dress it up a bit by using some Madeira (which is also used in the Mushroom–Shallot Toasts recipe on p. 89).

1	Tbsp canola oil
1 1/2	lb trimmed boneless chuck roast, cut into 4 pieces*
2	medium onions (4 oz each), cut into eighths
1	lb whole mushrooms
3/4	cup dry red wine or Madeira
1	Tbsp Worcestershire sauce
2	tsp dried thyme
1	tsp instant coffee granules
1/2	tsp ground allspice
1/2	tsp black pepper
2	Tbsp water
1	Tbsp cornstarch
3/4	tsp salt

1 Press the Sauté button, then press the Adjust button to "More" or "High." When the display says "Hot," add the oil and tilt the pot to lightly coat the bottom. Add the beef and cook for 3 minutes on each side.

2 Top with the onions and mushrooms; add the wine and Worcestershire sauce. Sprinkle with the thyme, coffee granules, allspice, and pepper. Seal the lid, close the valve, press the Cancel button, and set to Manual/Pressure Cook for 60 minutes.

3 Use a quick pressure release. When the valve drops, carefully remove the lid. Remove the beef with a slotted spoon and set aside. Press the Cancel button and reset to Sauté. Then press the Adjust button to "More" or "High."

*When purchasing beef or pork, always buy about 8 oz more than you need. You will lose some of the weight after the meat is trimmed of fat.

4 In a small bowl, combine the water with the cornstarch and stir until the cornstarch is completely dissolved. Stir into the cooking liquid in the pot. Bring to a boil and boil for 10 minutes, or until reduced slightly, stirring frequently. Stir in the beef and the salt.

NUTRITION FACTS

Choices/Exchanges: 2 Nonstarchy Vegetable, 4 Lean Protein, 1/2 Fat

Calories: 250; Calories from Fat: 90; Total Fat: 10.0 g; Saturated Fat: 2.5 g; Trans Fat: 0.3 g; Cholesterol: 85 mg; Sodium: 440 mg; Potassium: 720 mg; Total Carbohydrate: 10 g; Dietary Fiber: 2 g; Sugars: 4 g; Protein: 31 g; Phosphorus: 300 mg

4-Ingredient Salsa Verde Pork

SERVES: 8   **SERVING SIZE:** 1/2 cup pork   **HANDS-ON TIME:** 18 minutes   **HANDS-OFF TIME:** 45 minutes
TOTAL TIME: 1 hour and 3 minutes

Cook this today, but *wait!* This is a fantastically flavorful "make-ahead" entrée. It tastes even better the next day and freezes well, too!

Nonstick cooking spray
2 lb trimmed boneless pork shoulder steak, cut into 1-inch cubes*
1 1/2 cups salsa verde (such as Pace)
1/2 cup water
1/4 tsp salt
1/2 cup chopped fresh cilantro or green onion
2 limes, cut into 8 wedges total

1. Press the Sauté button, then press the Adjust button to "More" or "High." When the display says "Hot," liberally coat the Instant Pot with cooking spray. Working in 2 batches, add half of the pork in a single layer to the pot and cook for 5 minutes, and do not stir. Remove and set aside. Coat the browned bits in the pot with cooking spray and repeat with the remaining pork.

2. Return the pork to the pot, and stir in the salsa verde and water. Seal the lid, close the valve, press the Cancel button, and set to Manual/Pressure Cook for 30 minutes.

3. Use a natural pressure release for 10 minutes, followed by a quick pressure release. When the valve drops, carefully remove the lid. Stir in the salt.

*When purchasing beef or pork, always buy about 8 oz more than you need. You will lose some of the weight after the meat is trimmed of fat.

4 Press the Cancel button and reset to Sauté. Then press the Adjust button to "More" or "High." Bring to a boil and boil for 5 minutes to thicken.

5 The flavor of the dish improves if you refrigerate it overnight. At the time of serving, sprinkle with cilantro and serve with the lime wedges to squeeze over all.

NUTRITION FACTS

Choices/Exchanges: 3 Lean Protein, 1 Fat

Calories: 190; Calories from Fat: 80; Total Fat: 9.0 g; Saturated Fat: 2.9 g; Trans Fat: 0.0 g; Cholesterol: 70 mg; Sodium: 310 mg; Potassium: 440 mg; Total Carbohydrate: 3 g; Dietary Fiber: 1 g; Sugars: 2 g; Protein: 23 g; Phosphorus: 210 mg

No-Need-to-Brown Meatballs and Sauce

SERVES: 6 **SERVING SIZE:** 4 meatballs and about 1/2 cup sauce **HANDS-ON TIME:** 15 minutes
HANDS-OFF TIME: 15 minutes **TOTAL TIME:** 30 minutes

Looking to save steps whenever you can? Skip the browning this time! Most of us tend to think that meatballs should be browned first, which can be time-consuming and sometimes tricky! No need to in this recipe—absolutely no need!

1	lb extra-lean (95% lean) ground beef
2/3	cups quick-cooking or rolled oats
1/3	cup finely chopped onion
3	Tbsp dried basil, divided
2	tsp dried Italian seasoning
1/4	tsp garlic powder
1/4	tsp crushed pepper flakes
2	eggs
3/4	cup dry red wine
1	(28-oz) can no-salt-added crushed tomatoes
1	Tbsp sugar
2	Tbsp tomato paste
3/4	tsp salt
2	Tbsp grated Parmesan cheese

1 In a large bowl, combine the beef with the oats, onion, 1 1/2 Tbsp of the basil, the Italian seasoning, garlic powder, pepper flakes, and eggs. Shape into 24 meatballs.

2 Add the wine to the Instant Pot and arrange the meatballs in a single layer in the pot.

3 In the same bowl the meatballs were in, combine the crushed tomatoes, remaining basil, the sugar, tomato paste, and salt. Stir until well blended and pour evenly over the meatballs. Do not stir.

4 Seal the lid, close the valve, and set the Manual/Pressure Cook button to 5 minutes.

5 Use a quick pressure release. When the valve drops, carefully remove the lid and sprinkle cheese evenly over all.

COOK'S NOTE

These meatballs are even better the next day! Serve as is or over cooked veggie spirals.

NUTRITION FACTS

Choices/Exchanges: 1/2 Starch, 2 Nonstarchy Vegetable, 2 Lean Protein, 1 Fat
Calories: 240; Calories from Fat: 60; Total Fat: 7.0 g; Saturated Fat: 2.7 g;
Trans Fat: 0.1 g; Cholesterol: 110 mg; Sodium: 390 mg; Potassium: 780 mg;
Total Carbohydrate: 18 g; Dietary Fiber: 4 g; Sugars: 8 g; Protein: 22 g;
Phosphorus: 270 mg

Sides: Starchy and Nonstarchy

8

Smoky Petite Potatoes
page 144

**Artichokes with
Fresh Lemon Oil**
page 145

Acorn Squash with Raisins and Toasted Pecans

SERVES: 4 **SERVING SIZE:** 1 squash wedge and 2 Tbsp pecan mixture **HANDS-ON TIME:** 15 minutes
HANDS-OFF TIME: 20 minutes **TOTAL TIME:** 35 minutes

The natural juices from the squash are released during the pressurized cooking process, and when the other ingredients are added at the end, it makes a filling that is crunchy, nutty, and has a fruity natural sweetness.

1/4 cup chopped pecans
1/4 cup raisins
1/4 cup finely chopped red onion
1 tsp grated orange zest
1/4 tsp salt
1 cup water
1 lb acorn squash, cut into fourths and seeds removed

1 Press the Sauté button, then press the Adjust button to "More" or "High." When the display says "Hot," add the pecans to the Instant Pot. Cook for 4 minutes, stirring occasionally. Remove the pecans, place them in a medium bowl, and add the raisins, onion, orange zest, and salt.

2 Place the water in the Instant Pot. Top with a steamer basket. Arrange the squash in the steamer basket, skin side down. Seal the lid, close the valve, and press the Cancel button. Set to Manual/Pressure Cook for 5 minutes.

3 Use a natural pressure release for 10 minutes, followed by a quick pressure release. When the valve drops, carefully remove the lid. Remove the squash wedges. Spoon an equal amount of the pecan mixture on top of each squash wedge.

COOK'S NOTE

To cut the squash easily, pierce the squash over the entire surface with the tip of a sharp knife. Place in the microwave and set on high for 2 minutes. Using 2 dish towels or pot holders, remove the squash carefully from the microwave (it will be hot). Let cool for 1 minute before cutting.

COOK'S NOTE

For an extra kick, add 1/8 teaspoon of crushed pepper flakes to the pecan mixture.

NUTRITION FACTS

Choices/Exchanges: 1 Starch, 1/2 Fruit, 1/2 Fat

Calories: 120; Calories from Fat: 45; Total Fat: 5.0 g; Saturated Fat: 0.5 g; Trans Fat: 0.0 g; Cholesterol: 0 mg; Sodium: 150 mg; Potassium: 490 mg; Total Carbohydrate: 21 g; Dietary Fiber: 3 g; Sugars: 6 g; Protein: 2 g; Phosphorus: 70 mg

Fast and Fresh Corn on the Cob

SERVES: 4   **SERVING SIZE:** 1 ear corn and about 2 tsp butter mixture   **HANDS-ON TIME:** 6 minutes
HANDS-OFF TIME: 8 minutes   **TOTAL TIME:** 14 minutes

No hot pots of water steaming up the already hot kitchen. No need to pour boiling water down the sink after the corn is cooked. None of that. Just pressure cook for 3 minutes and enjoy!

1 cup water
4 large ears of corn, shucked
3 Tbsp light butter with canola oil
1 tsp black pepper
1/4 tsp salt
1 Tbsp finely chopped fresh parsley

1. Place the water in the Instant Pot. Top with a trivet. Place the ears of corn on the trivet, overlapping slightly. Seal the lid, close the valve, and set the Manual/Pressure Cook button to 3 minutes.

2. Use a quick pressure release. Meanwhile, combine the butter, pepper, and salt in a small bowl and set aside.

3. When the valve drops, carefully remove the lid. Remove the corn with tongs and top each with equal amounts of the butter mixture. Sprinkle with the parsley.

NUTRITION FACTS

Choices/Exchanges: 1 1/2 Starch, 1 Fat

Calories: 150; Calories from Fat: 50; Total Fat: 6.0 g; Saturated Fat: 1.7 g;
Trans Fat: 0.0 g; Cholesterol: 10 mg; Sodium: 210 mg; Potassium: 280 mg;
Total Carbohydrate: 25 g; Dietary Fiber: 3 g; Sugars: 5 g; Protein: 4 g;
Phosphorus: 95 mg

Lemon–Basil Pesto Farro

SERVES: 4   **SERVING SIZE:** 1/2 cup   **HANDS-ON TIME:** 5 minutes   **HANDS-OFF TIME:** 13 minutes
TOTAL TIME: 18 minutes

Farro is an ancient wheat grain that is becoming increasingly popular with home cooks because of its high fiber and protein content. It has an appearance similar to brown rice when cooked, but it is chewier in texture and has a nutty flavor. It can be used on its own as you would rice or multigrain pasta, or tossed into salads and soups. It is sold in major supermarkets and health food stores.

3/4	cup uncooked pearled farro
2	tsp extra-virgin olive oil
2	cups water
3	Tbsp basil pesto (such as Classico)
2	tsp grated lemon zest
1	Tbsp lemon juice
1/8	tsp salt

1. Combine the farro, oil, and water in the Instant Pot. Seal the lid, close the valve, and set the Manual/Pressure Cook button to 7 minutes.

2. Use a quick pressure release. When the valve drops, carefully remove the lid. Turn off the heat. Place the farro in a fine mesh sieve and drain well.

3. Return the drained farro to the pot and combine with the remaining ingredients, tossing until well blended. Serve immediately for peak flavors.

NUTRITION FACTS

Choices/Exchanges: 2 Starch, 1 Fat

Calories: 190; Calories from Fat: 60; Total Fat: 7.0 g; Saturated Fat: 1.2 g; Trans Fat: 0.0 g; Cholesterol: 0 mg; Sodium: 180 mg; Potassium: 150 mg; Total Carbohydrate: 28 g; Dietary Fiber: 4 g; Sugars: 0 g; Protein: 6 g; Phosphorus: 160 mg

Creamy Garlic–Basil Pasta

SERVES: 4   **SERVING SIZE:** 1/2 cup   **HANDS-ON TIME:** 7 minutes   **HANDS-OFF TIME:** 9 minutes
TOTAL TIME: 16 minutes

Sometimes you need a simple pasta dish to serve alongside a simple (or not-so-simple) entrée. This side has simplicity *and* personality! The multigrain pasta has a lot of fiber but is lighter in texture than the whole-wheat varieties.

- 4 oz uncooked multigrain rotini pasta (such as Barilla Protein Plus)
- 3 cups water
- 2 garlic cloves, peeled
- 1 tsp extra-virgin olive oil
- 1 oz reduced-fat cream cheese, cut into small pieces
- 3 Tbsp chopped fresh basil
- 1/4 tsp salt
- 1/4 tsp black pepper
- 2 Tbsp grated Parmesan cheese
- 1 cup chopped green onion (both green and white parts)

1 Combine the pasta, water, garlic, and oil in the Instant Pot. Stir, making sure the pasta is covered in water. Seal the lid, close the valve, and set the Manual/Pressure Cook button to 3 minutes.

2 Use a quick pressure release. When the valve drops, carefully remove the lid. Place a colander over a bowl and drain the pasta, reserving 1/4 cup of the cooking liquid.

3 Place the garlic back in the pot and mash with a fork. Return the pasta to the pot with the reserved 1/4 cup of liquid, the cream cheese, basil, salt, and pepper. Stir until the cream cheese has melted, then sprinkle with the Parmesan cheese and green onion.

NUTRITION FACTS

Choices/Exchanges: 1 1/2 Starch, 1/2 Fat

Calories: 140; Calories from Fat: 35; Total Fat: 4.0 g; Saturated Fat: 1.5 g; Trans Fat: 0.0 g; Cholesterol: 5 mg; Sodium: 220 mg; Potassium: 200 mg; Total Carbohydrate: 21 g; Dietary Fiber: 3 g; Sugars: 2 g; Protein: 7 g; Phosphorus: 120 mg

"Baked" Sweet Potatoes with Honey'd Pecans

SERVES: 4   **SERVING SIZE:** 1 potato half (6 oz) and 1 Tbsp nut mixture   **HANDS-ON TIME:** 11 minutes
HANDS-OFF TIME: 29 minutes   **TOTAL TIME:** 40 minutes

Pressure cooking locks in the flavors of foods, but it also locks in the natural moisture, which is especially helpful when cooking sweet potatoes as they can sometimes become dry.

1/4 cup chopped pecans
1 Tbsp honey
1/2 tsp cake batter flavor or vanilla extract (such as McCormick)
1/8 tsp ground nutmeg
1/8 tsp salt
1 cup water
2 (12-oz) sweet potatoes, cut in half lengthwise

1 Press the Sauté button, then press the Adjust button to "More" or "High." When the display says "Hot," add the nuts to the Instant Pot and cook for 4 minutes, stirring occasionally. Remove the nuts and place in a small bowl with the honey, cake batter flavor, nutmeg, and salt; set aside.

2 Place the water in the Instant Pot. Top with a trivet. Wrap each potato half with foil and arrange potatoes on the trivet. Seal the lid, close the valve, and press the Cancel button. Set to Manual/Pressure Cook for 12 minutes.

3 Use a natural pressure release for about 12 minutes. When the valve drops, carefully remove the lid. Remove the potatoes and carefully unwrap. Fluff each potato half with a fork. Spoon equal amounts of the pecan mixture on top of each potato half.

NUTRITION FACTS

Choices/Exchanges: 2 Starch, 1/2 Fat

Calories: 180; Calories from Fat: 45; Total Fat: 5.0 g; Saturated Fat: 0.5 g; Trans Fat: 0.0 g; Cholesterol: 0 mg; Sodium: 115 mg; Potassium: 380 mg; Total Carbohydrate: 32 g; Dietary Fiber: 4 g; Sugars: 13 g; Protein: 3 g; Phosphorus: 70 mg

Smoky Petite Potatoes

SERVES: 6   **SERVING SIZE:** 3/4 cup   **HANDS-ON TIME:** 10 minutes   **HANDS-OFF TIME:** 14 minutes
TOTAL TIME: 24 minutes (plus 10 minutes standing time)

These tender little potatoes have the appearance of your typical roasted potatoes, but they have moisture trapped deep inside by the pressure-cooking process and are bursting with smoky flavors!

1   cup water
1 1/2 lb petite potatoes
       (each about
       1 1/2 inches in
       diameter)
1   cup chopped green
       onion (both green
       and white parts)
1   tsp smoked paprika
2   Tbsp extra-virgin
       olive oil
1/2 tsp garlic powder
1/8 tsp black pepper
1/2 tsp salt

1 Place the water in the Instant Pot. Top with a steamer basket. Arrange the potatoes in the steamer basket. Seal the lid, close the valve, and set the Manual/Pressure Cook button to 8 minutes.

2 Use a quick pressure release. When the valve drops, carefully remove the lid. Remove the potatoes and discard the water.

3 Press the Cancel button and set to Sauté. Then press the Adjust button to "More" or "High." Return the potatoes to the pot with the remaining ingredients. Cook for 3 minutes, or until beginning to lightly brown, stirring occasionally.

4 Place the potatoes in a bowl and let stand for 10 minutes before serving for peak flavors and texture. Serve hot or at room temperature.

NUTRITION FACTS

Choices/Exchanges: 1 1/2 Starch, 1/2 Fat

Calories: 140; Calories from Fat: 40; Total Fat: 4.5 g; Saturated Fat: 0.6 g; Trans Fat: 0.0 g; Cholesterol: 0 mg; Sodium: 110 mg; Potassium: 690 mg; Total Carbohydrate: 22 g; Dietary Fiber: 3 g; Sugars: 2 g; Protein: 3 g; Phosphorus: 65 mg

Artichokes with Fresh Lemon Oil

SERVES: 4   **SERVING SIZE:** 1 artichoke half and 1 tsp sauce   **HANDS-ON TIME:** 12 minutes
HANDS-OFF TIME: 22 minutes   **TOTAL TIME:** 34 minutes

Do you love fresh artichokes? Have you ever tasted or tried to cook a fresh artichoke? Well, now you don't have to wait, wonder, or waver! These artichokes are *so* easy! They're also pretty and perfectly seasoned to let the natural flavor of the artichoke come through. Just a little prep—not a lot—and you're ready to enjoy!

2   medium artichokes, trimmed*
1/2 cup dry white wine
1/2 cup water
1/2 lemon
1/2 tsp dried oregano

Sauce:
1   Tbsp extra-virgin olive oil
1   tsp hot sauce (such as Frank's RedHot)
1/2 tsp grated lemon zest
1   tsp lemon juice
1/8 tsp salt
1   lemon, cut into 4 wedges

1 Cut each artichoke in half lengthwise. Using a spoon, scrape out the fuzzy choke portion and discard.

2 Pour the wine and water into the Instant Pot. Top with a steamer basket. Arrange the artichoke halves with the cut side up in the basket. Squeeze the juice of the lemon half over all and sprinkle with oregano.

3 Seal the lid, close the valve, and set the Manual/Pressure Cook button to 15 minutes.

4 Use a quick pressure release. Meanwhile, combine all the sauce ingredients, except for the salt and lemon wedges, in a small bowl.

5 When the valve drops, carefully remove the lid. Transfer the artichokes to a platter, cut side up. Drizzle the sauce evenly over the artichokes and sprinkle with the salt. Serve with the lemon wedges to squeeze over all.

*To trim artichokes, peel off and discard the tough outer leaves, and cut about 1 inch off the top. Using scissors, snip off any prickly ends of the artichoke leaves.

NUTRITION FACTS

Choices/Exchanges: 2 Nonstarchy Vegetable, 1/2 Fat

Calories: 70; Calories from Fat: 30; Total Fat: 3.5 g; Saturated Fat: 0.5 g;
Trans Fat: 0.0 g; Cholesterol: 0 mg; Sodium: 160 mg; Potassium: 200 mg;
Total Carbohydrate: 9 g; Dietary Fiber: 4 g; Sugars: 1 g; Protein: 2 g; Phosphorus: 45 mg

Chipotle Yellow Rice with Red Peppers

SERVES: 4   **SERVING SIZE:** About 3/4 cup   **HANDS-ON TIME:** 6 minutes   **HANDS-OFF TIME:** 31 minutes
TOTAL TIME: 37 minutes

Adding turmeric to the water allows the rice to absorb it while cooking so the rice pops with a bright yellow color when done!

1	cup water
3/4	cup brown rice, rinsed
1/2	tsp ground turmeric
1/2	chipotle chile pepper (canned in adobo sauce), minced
1 1/2	cups chopped red bell pepper
1	Tbsp extra-virgin olive oil
1/8	tsp and 1/4 tsp salt, divided

1 Combine all the ingredients, except 1/4 tsp of the salt, in the Instant Pot. Seal the lid, close the valve, and set the Manual/Pressure Cook button to 15 minutes.

2 Use a natural pressure release for 10 minutes, followed by a quick pressure release. When the valve drops, carefully remove the lid. Stir in the remaining salt and serve.

NUTRITION FACTS

Choices/Exchanges: 1 1/2 Starch, 1 Nonstarchy Vegetable, 1 Fat

Calories: 180; Calories from Fat: 40; Total Fat: 4.5 g; Saturated Fat: 0.7 g; Trans Fat: 0.0 g; Cholesterol: 0 mg; Sodium: 230 mg; Potassium: 210 mg; Total Carbohydrate: 30 g; Dietary Fiber: 3 g; Sugars: 3 g; Protein: 3 g; Phosphorus: 125 mg

Glazed Beets and Carrots

SERVES: 4 **SERVING SIZE:** 1/2 cup **HANDS-ON TIME:** 13 minutes **HANDS-OFF TIME:** 24 minutes
TOTAL TIME: 37 minutes

Afraid of beets staining your fingers? Don't worry, just be sure to peel the beets under running water. That's all you have to do to prevent your fingers from staining!

1 cup water
3 medium beets (about 3 oz each), rinsed
2 medium carrots (about 3 oz each), rinsed
1 Tbsp sugar
2 Tbsp orange juice
1 Tbsp extra-virgin olive oil
1/8 tsp salt
1/2 tsp grated orange zest

1 Place the water in the Instant Pot. Top with a steamer basket. Arrange the beets and carrots in the steamer basket. Seal the lid, close the valve, and set the Manual/Pressure Cook button to 18 minutes.

2 Use a quick pressure release. When the valve drops, carefully remove the lid. Place the beets in a colander. Run under cold water until cool enough to handle.

3 Hold 1 beet under running water while slipping the peel off with your fingertips. Place on a paper towel and repeat with the remaining beets. Cut each beet into 8 wedges.

4 Remove the carrots from the pot and cut into thirds.

5 Remove the steamer basket from the pot and discard the water. Press the Cancel button and set to Sauté. Then press the Adjust button to "More" or "High." Add the sugar, orange juice, oil, and salt. Stir in the beets and cook for 2 minutes, or until glazed. Add the carrots, stir, and cook for 30 seconds, or until well coated. Stir in the orange zest.

NUTRITION FACTS
Choices/Exchanges: 2 Nonstarchy Vegetable, 1 Fat
Calories: 90; Calories from Fat: 30; Total Fat: 3.5 g; Saturated Fat: 0.5 g;
Trans Fat: 0.0 g; Cholesterol: 0 mg; Sodium: 140 mg; Potassium: 290 mg;
Total Carbohydrate: 13 g; Dietary Fiber: 2 g; Sugars: 10 g; Protein: 1 g;
Phosphorus: 35 mg

Cabbage Wedges with Bacon

SERVES: 4　　**SERVING SIZE:** 1 wedge (about 3/4 cup)　　**HANDS-ON TIME:** 14 minutes
HANDS-OFF TIME: 11 minutes　　**TOTAL TIME:** 25 minutes

A wedge of cabbage adds a bit of comfort to a meal, especially if there's a chill in the air. Normally, though, the water soluble vitamins in cabbage get lost if it's cooked in a lot of water. And steamed cabbage doesn't really bring home the comfort, does it? Pressure cooking locks in that familiar flavor of the cabbage. When combined with the technique I use to concentrate the liquid at the end of cooking, well . . . I just hope you're hungry!

1　oz uncooked bacon
　　slices
1　lb green cabbage,
　　cut into 4 wedges
1　cup water
1/8　tsp salt
1/8　tsp black pepper

1　Press the Sauté button, then press the Adjust button to "More" or "High." When the display says "Hot," add the bacon and cook for 4 minutes, or until browned. Drain the bacon slices on paper towels and tear into small pieces.

2　To the bacon drippings, add the cabbage wedges (cut side down) and water; sprinkle evenly with the salt and pepper and top with the bacon pieces. Seal the lid, close the valve, and press the Cancel button. Set to Manual/Pressure Cook for 7 minutes.

3　Use a quick pressure release. When the valve drops, carefully remove the lid. Remove the cabbage with a slotted spoon. Set aside on a plate.

4 Press the Cancel button and reset to Sauté. Then press the Adjust button to "More" or "High." Bring to a boil and boil for 2–3 minutes, or until reduced to 2 Tbsp of liquid.

5 Spoon the liquid over the cabbage.

NUTRITION FACTS

Choices/Exchanges: 1 Nonstarchy Vegetable, 1/2 Fat

Calories: 50; Calories from Fat: 25; Total Fat: 3.0 g; Saturated Fat: 1.0 g;
Trans Fat: 0.0 g; Cholesterol: 3 mg; Sodium: 135 mg; Potassium: 170 mg;
Total Carbohydrate: 5 g; Dietary Fiber: 2 g; Sugars: 3 g; Protein: 2 g;
Phosphorus: 35 mg

Hot-or-Cold Fresh Herb Carrots

SERVES: 4   **SERVING SIZE:** 3 carrot pieces   **HANDS-ON TIME:** 5 minutes   **HANDS-OFF TIME:** 8 minutes
TOTAL TIME: 13 minutes (plus 15 minutes standing time or 1 hour chill time)

Serve 'em hot for a side vegetable or serve 'em cold as a refreshing side or salad. You could also cut the carrots in half again and serve them as an appetizer with wooden toothpicks! Be sure to serve them the same day—preferably within 4 hours—for peak flavors.

1 cup water
6 medium carrots (about 1 lb total), ends trimmed and carrots cut in half crosswise to make 12 pieces total
2 Tbsp white balsamic vinegar
1 Tbsp canola oil
1 tsp sugar
1/8 tsp salt
1/4 cup chopped fresh mint, basil, or cilantro

1 Place the water in the Instant Pot. Top with a steamer basket. Arrange the carrots in the steamer basket. Seal the lid, close the valve, and set the Manual/Pressure Cook button to 2 minutes.

2 Use a quick pressure release. When the valve drops, carefully remove the lid. Place the carrots on a rimmed platter or in a 13 x 9-inch casserole dish in a single layer. Drizzle the vinegar and oil over the carrots and sprinkle with the sugar, salt, and mint.

3 Let stand for 15 minutes to serve at room temperature or refrigerate for 1 hour to serve chilled.

NUTRITION FACTS

Choices/Exchanges: 2 Nonstarchy Vegetable, 1 Fat

Calories: 90; Calories from Fat: 35; Total Fat: 4.0 g; Saturated Fat: 0.3 g; Trans Fat: 0.0 g; Cholesterol: 0 mg; Sodium: 150 mg; Potassium: 370 mg; Total Carbohydrate: 14 g; Dietary Fiber: 3 g; Sugars: 8 g; Protein: 1 g; Phosphorus: 40 mg

Garlic–Herb Cauliflower Mash

SERVES: 4   **SERVING SIZE:** 1/2 cup   **HANDS-ON TIME:** 6 minutes   **HANDS-OFF TIME:** 11 minutes
TOTAL TIME: 17 minutes

This side dish is ridiculously easy—and *fast*, of course! Just pop the cauliflower and peeled garlic (no mincing!) into the pot, cook, drain, do a quick mash, and top with olive oil and Parmesan. See? Easy!

1	cup water
16	oz fresh or frozen cauliflower florets
1	garlic clove, peeled
1/2	tsp dried oregano
4	tsp extra-virgin olive oil
1/8	tsp salt
1/8	tsp black pepper
4	tsp grated Parmesan cheese

1 Place the water in the Instant Pot. Top with a steamer basket. Arrange the cauliflower and garlic in the steamer basket. Sprinkle with the oregano. Seal the lid, close the valve, and set the Manual/Pressure Cook button to 5 minutes.

2 Use a quick pressure release. When the valve drops, carefully remove the lid. Turn off the Instant Pot. Remove the cauliflower mixture and the steamer basket from the pot. Discard the water and return the cauliflower and garlic to the pot.

3 Mash the cauliflower and garlic with a potato masher or electric mixer. Drizzle the oil evenly over the mash. Sprinkle evenly with the salt, pepper, and cheese. Do not stir.

NUTRITION FACTS

Choices/Exchanges: 1 Nonstarchy Vegetable, 1 Fat

Calories: 80; Calories from Fat: 45; Total Fat: 5.0 g; Saturated Fat: 1.0 g;
Trans Fat: 0.0 g; Cholesterol: 0 mg; Sodium: 125 mg; Potassium: 350 mg;
Total Carbohydrate: 6 g; Dietary Fiber: 2 g; Sugars: 2 g; Protein: 3 g;
Phosphorus: 60 mg

Cauliflower Wedges with Delicate Cheese Sauce

SERVES: 4   **SERVING SIZE:** 1 wedge (about 1 cup) and 2 Tbsp sauce   **HANDS-ON TIME:** 10 minutes
HANDS-OFF TIME: 10 minutes   **TOTAL TIME:** 20 minutes

Wedges of *anything* always look inviting and add character to the dish. But if you make a sauce for those wedges, it can be loaded with saturated fat and sodium. Not in this recipe! This sauce is all about the cheese—2 cheeses to be exact—and the way they're used!

1   large head cauliflower (about 6–7 inches in diameter; about 1 1/2 lb total)
1   cup water
1/2   cup 2% milk
1 1/2   tsp cornstarch
1   oz shredded reduced-fat sharp cheddar cheese
1/2   oz crumbled reduced-fat blue cheese
1/8   tsp black pepper

1   Trim the leaves and most of the core from the cauliflower, but leave enough of the core to keep the cauliflower head intact.

2   Place the water and a trivet in the Instant Pot. Place the whole cauliflower head on the trivet. Seal the lid, close the valve, and set the Manual/Pressure Cook button to 3 minutes.

3   Use a quick pressure release. When the valve drops, carefully remove the lid. Using 2 large spoons, carefully remove the cauliflower and place it on a platter. Remove the trivet and discard the water.

4   In a small bowl, whisk together the milk and cornstarch.

5 Press the Cancel button and set to Sauté. Then press the Adjust button to "More" or "High." Add the milk mixture to the Instant Pot. Bring to a boil and boil for 1 minute, or until thickened, stirring frequently. Gradually add the cheeses and stir until melted.

6 Spoon the sauce on top of the cauliflower and sprinkle with the pepper. Cut the cauliflower into 4 wedges and serve.

NUTRITION FACTS

Choices/Exchanges: 1 Nonstarchy Vegetable, 1 Fat

Calories: 80; Calories from Fat: 25; Total Fat: 3.0 g; Saturated Fat: 1.7 g; Trans Fat: 0.0 g; Cholesterol: 10 mg; Sodium: 140 mg; Potassium: 360 mg; Total Carbohydrate: 8 g; Dietary Fiber: 2 g; Sugars: 4 g; Protein: 6 g; Phosphorus: 130 mg

Chia–Berry Crepes
page 160

Pumpkin Bread Pudding with Apple–Vanilla Sauce

page 166

Almond and Toffee–Topped Pears

SERVES: 4 **SERVING SIZE:** 1 pear half and about 4 tsp almond mixture **HANDS-ON TIME:** 15 minutes **HANDS-OFF TIME:** 11 minutes **TOTAL TIME:** 26 minutes

Boiling down (or reducing) the liquid at the end of the cooking time concentrates the natural juices and spices. Adding the crushed candies gives the liquid a butterscotch or toffee flavor!

1/4 cup slivered almonds

8 sugar-free caramel-flavored hard candies (such as Werther's Original), crushed in a plastic bag

1/16 tsp salt

3/4 cup water

1/4 cup apple juice

1 cinnamon stick

2 **firm** pears (8 oz each), peeled, halved lengthwise, and cored

1 tsp light butter with canola oil

1/2 tsp vanilla extract

1 Press the Sauté button, then press the Adjust button to "More" or "High." When the display says "Hot," add the almonds to the Instant Pot and cook for 4 minutes, stirring occasionally. Remove from the pot and set aside to cool.

2 Coarsely chop the almonds and add to the crushed candies and salt in a small bowl. Set aside.

3 Place the water, apple juice, and cinnamon stick in the Instant Pot. Top with a steamer basket. Arrange the pears in the steamer basket. Seal the lid, close the valve, and press the Cancel button. Set to Manual/Pressure Cook for 2 minutes. (If you prefer a very tender pear, cook for 1 additional minute.)

4 Use a quick pressure release. When the valve drops, carefully remove the lid. Remove the steamer basket and pears. Place the pears, cut side up, in four dessert bowls. Remove and discard the cinnamon stick.

5 Press the Cancel button and reset to Sauté. Then press the Adjust button to "More" or "High." Bring the cooking liquid to a boil and boil for 3 minutes, or until reduced to 1/4 cup of liquid. Stir in the butter, vanilla extract, and almonds and crushed candies. Cook for 30 seconds, or until the candies have melted, stirring constantly.

6 Working quickly, spoon equal amounts of the almond mixture in the center of each pear half.

NUTRITION FACTS

Choices/Exchanges: 1 Fruit, 1/2 Carbohydrate, 1 Fat

Calories: 130; Calories from Fat: 45; Total Fat: 5.0 g; Saturated Fat: 0.9 g; Trans Fat: 0.0 g; Cholesterol: 5 mg; Sodium: 80 mg; Potassium: 170 mg; Total Carbohydrate: 22 g; Dietary Fiber: 4 g; Sugars: 11 g; Protein: 2 g; Phosphorus: 45 mg

Chia–Berry Crepes

SERVES: 4   **SERVING SIZE:** 1 crepe with about 1/3 cup berry mixture and 1/4 cup yogurt
HANDS-ON TIME: 7 minutes   **HANDS-OFF TIME:** 6 minutes   **TOTAL TIME:** 13 minutes
(plus 15 minutes standing time)

Those teeny chia seeds are loaded with fiber, and when mixed with liquids they become gelatinous so they help to thicken sauces, dressings, etc. Keep that in mind when you want to incorporate more fiber—and texture—into your meals.

- 1 cup frozen blueberries
- 1 cup frozen raspberries
- 1/2 cup plus 1 Tbsp water, divided
- 2 tsp chia seeds
- 2 tsp cornstarch
- 3 Tbsp powdered sugar, divided
- 1/8 tsp almond extract
- 4 premade crepes (such as Melissa's)
- 1 cup plain 2% Greek yogurt (such as Fage)

1 Place the berries, 1/2 cup of the water, and the chia seeds in the Instant Pot. Seal the lid, close the valve, and set the Manual/Pressure Cook button to 1 minute.

2 Use a quick pressure release. When the valve drops, carefully remove the lid.

3 In a small bowl, stir together the remaining 1 Tbsp of water and the cornstarch. Stir until the cornstarch is dissolved.

4 Press the Cancel button and set to Sauté. Then press the Adjust button to "More" or "High." Stir the cornstarch mixture into the berries. Bring to a boil and boil for 1 minute, or until thickened slightly.

5 Turn off the heat. Stir in 2 Tbsp of the powdered sugar and the almond extract. Place the berry mixture in a medium bowl and let stand for 15 minutes to cool slightly.

6 Spoon equal amounts of the berry mixture down the center of each crepe. Fold the ends over to overlap slightly. Spoon the remaining 1 Tbsp of powdered sugar into a fine mesh sieve and sprinkle evenly over each crepe. Top each crepe with an equal amount of the yogurt. Serve warm or chilled, if desired.

NUTRITION FACTS

Choices/Exchanges: 1 Starch, 1/2 Fruit, 1/2 Carbohydrate, 1 Lean Protein

Calories: 170; Calories from Fat: 30; Total Fat: 3.5 g; Saturated Fat: 1.2 g; Trans Fat: 0.0 g; Cholesterol: 10 mg; Sodium: 105 mg; Potassium: 190 mg; Total Carbohydrate: 28 g; Dietary Fiber: 4 g; Sugars: 17 g; Protein: 8 g; Phosphorus: 130 mg

Strawberry–Pear Applesauce with Ginger

SERVES: 8   **SERVING SIZE:** 3/4 cup   **HANDS-ON TIME:** 15 minutes   **HANDS-OFF TIME:** 37 minutes
TOTAL TIME: 52 minutes (plus 8 hours chill time)

This is not your typical applesauce. It's packed with fiber, a variety of fresh fruits, fresh and dried spices, and a tip of vanilla! Serve it with breakfast items, as a midday snack, or as a dessert. It lasts up to a month in the refrigerator, too. So it's there for you for a long time!

- 1 lb apples (such as Gala or Honeycrisp), halved, cored, and cut into 1-inch chunks
- 1 lb **ripe** pears, halved, cored, and cut into 1-inch chunks
- 1 lb fresh strawberries, stems removed
- 2/3 cup pear nectar
- 1/4 tsp ground cinnamon
- 1/8 tsp salt
- 2 Tbsp sugar
- 1 Tbsp grated fresh ginger
- 2 tsp lemon juice
- 1 tsp vanilla extract

1 Place the apples, pears, strawberries, pear nectar, cinnamon, and salt in the Instant Pot. Seal the lid, close the valve, and set the Manual/Pressure Cook button to 5 minutes.

2 Use a natural pressure release for about 20 minutes. When the valve drops, carefully remove the lid. Stir in the sugar, ginger, lemon juice, and vanilla extract. Pour into a large bowl.

3 Cool the applesauce completely before covering and placing in the refrigerator. Refrigerate for at least 8 hours or overnight.

COOK'S NOTE
This sauce will thicken when completely cooled. It's even better the next day.

NUTRITION FACTS

Choices/Exchanges: 2 Fruit

Calories: 100; Calories from Fat: 0; Total Fat: 0.0 g; Saturated Fat: 0.0 g; Trans Fat: 0.0 g; Cholesterol: 0 mg; Sodium: 40 mg; Potassium: 210 mg; Total Carbohydrate: 26 g; Dietary Fiber: 4 g; Sugars: 18 g; Protein: 1 g; Phosphorus: 25 mg

Toasted Almond, Pineapple, and Peach Pots

SERVES: 6   **SERVING SIZE:** 1/2 cup   **HANDS-ON TIME:** 13 minutes   **HANDS-OFF TIME:** 10 minutes
TOTAL TIME: 23 minutes (plus 10 minutes standing time)

Whether you're curled up on the sofa, working diligently on your computer, or just enjoying the peace and quiet, these individual little pots full of "baked" fruits and glazed nuts will warm your heart and appeal to your sweet tooth.

3/4 cup sliced almonds
1 cup water
1 cup chopped **firm** pears
1 1/2 cups frozen pineapple chunks
1 cup frozen peach slices
2 Tbsp raisins
2 Tbsp sugar, divided
1/8 tsp salt
1/2 tsp almond extract

1 Press the Sauté button, then press the Adjust button to "More" or "High." When the display says "Hot," add the almonds to the Instant Pot and cook for 4 minutes, stirring occasionally. Remove and set aside on a plate.

2 Place the water in the Instant Pot. Top with a trivet.

3 Combine the fruit (pears, pineapple, and peaches), raisins, 1 Tbsp of the sugar, the salt, and almond extract in a medium bowl. Spoon equal amounts of the fruit mixture into 6 (6-oz) ramekins. Cover each ramekin with foil. Place 3 ramekins on top of the trivet and stack the remaining 3 ramekins on top. Seal the lid, close the valve, press the Cancel button, and set the Manual/Pressure Cook button to 5 minutes.

4 Use a quick pressure release. When the valve drops, carefully remove the lid. Remove the ramekins and unwrap. Top each ramekin with equal amounts of the almonds and sprinkle the remaining 1 Tbsp of sugar evenly over all. Let stand for 10 minutes to absorb the flavors.

NUTRITION FACTS

Choices/Exchanges: 1 1/2 Fruit, 1 Fat

Calories: 140; Calories from Fat: 50; Total Fat: 6.0 g; Saturated Fat: 0.5 g; Trans Fat: 0.0 g; Cholesterol: 0 mg; Sodium: 50 mg; Potassium: 230 mg; Total Carbohydrate: 21 g; Dietary Fiber: 3 g; Sugars: 15 g; Protein: 3 g; Phosphorus: 65 mg

Citrus, Pear, and Rice Pudding

SERVES: 6   **SERVING SIZE:** 1/2 cup rice mixture and 1/4 cup pears   **HANDS-ON TIME:** 10 minutes
HANDS-OFF TIME: 33 minutes   **TOTAL TIME:** 43 minutes

Rinsing the rice is usually recommended before adding it to the pot, but not in this recipe! You want the starchiness of the rice to add to the overall creaminess of the pudding. Serve this tasty dessert hot or cold.

1 1/2 cups chopped **ripe** pears	
1 1/3 cups water, divided	
1 Tbsp raisins	
1/2 tsp grated orange zest	
3/4 cup brown rice (do not rinse)	
1 1/2 tsp ground flaxseed	
1 cinnamon stick	
1/2 cup fat-free evaporated milk	
1 1/2 Tbsp sugar	
1 tsp vanilla extract	
1/4 tsp salt	

1 Press the Sauté button, then press the Adjust button to "More" or "High." When the display says "Hot," add the pears, 1/3 cup of the water, raisins, and orange zest. Bring to a boil and boil for 2 minutes or until the pears are just tender. Remove the pear mixture and set aside in a small bowl.

2 Combine the rice, flaxseed, remaining 1 cup of water, and the cinnamon stick in the Instant Pot. Seal the lid, close the valve, and press the Cancel button. Set to Manual/Pressure Cook for 20 minutes.

3 Use a natural pressure release for 10 minutes, followed by a quick pressure release. When the valve drops, carefully remove the lid. Remove the cinnamon stick and discard. Stir in the milk, sugar, vanilla extract, and salt. Spoon into bowls and top with the pear mixture.

NUTRITION FACTS

Choices/Exchanges: 1 Starch, 1/2 Fruit, 1/2 Carbohydrate

Calories: 150; Calories from Fat: 10; Total Fat: 1.0 g; Saturated Fat: 0.2 g;
Trans Fat: 0.0 g; Cholesterol: 0 mg; Sodium: 125 mg; Potassium: 190 mg;
Total Carbohydrate: 30 g; Dietary Fiber: 3 g; Sugars: 10 g; Protein: 4 g;
Phosphorus: 125 mg

Citrusy Ginger-Spiced Grog

SERVES: 8 **SERVING SIZE:** 1/2 cup **HANDS-ON TIME:** 6 minutes **HANDS-OFF TIME:** 28 minutes
TOTAL TIME: 34 minutes

Grogs and cold weather go hand in hand, but those delicious grogs can be packed with sugary carbs and empty calories—until now! The mixture of natural juices, high-flavored spices, and citrus peel combined with vanilla creates the perfect balance of flavor and fun!

1 1/2 cups apple juice
1 1/4 cups cranberry-
         raspberry juice
         (such as Ocean Spray
         Cran-Raspberry)
   3/4 cup pear juice
   1/2 cup water
     2 (3-inch) pieces peeled
         fresh ginger
     1 medium orange,
         cut into 8 wedges
   1/2 medium lemon
     6 whole cloves
     2 cinnamon sticks
     1 Tbsp vanilla extract

1 Combine all the ingredients, except the vanilla extract, in the Instant Pot.

2 Seal the lid, close the valve, and set the Manual/Pressure Cook button to 10 minutes.

3 Use a natural pressure release for 10 minutes, followed by a quick pressure release. When the valve drops, carefully remove the lid. Using a slotted spoon, remove the fruit pieces, ginger, and spices before serving. Stir in the vanilla extract and serve.

COOK'S NOTE

You can pierce the lemon's skin with the cloves to hold the cloves in place before adding them to the pot. It makes it easier to remove the cloves at the end of the cooking time.

NUTRITION FACTS

Choices/Exchanges: 1 Fruit

Calories: 60; Calories from Fat: 0; Total Fat: 0.0 g; Saturated Fat: 0.0 g; Trans Fat: 0.0 g; Cholesterol: 0 mg; Sodium: 10 mg; Potassium: 60 mg; Total Carbohydrate: 14 g; Dietary Fiber: 0 g; Sugars: 11 g; Protein: 0 g; Phosphorus: 5 mg

Pumpkin Bread Pudding with Apple–Vanilla Sauce

SERVES: 8   **SERVING SIZE:** 1/8 (1 wedge) bread pudding and 1 1/2 Tbsp sauce   **HANDS-ON TIME:** 20 minutes
HANDS-OFF TIME: 1 hour and 5 minutes   **TOTAL TIME:** 1 hour and 25 minutes (plus 25 minutes standing time)

Nothing says autumn like anything made with pumpkin. This moist, gorgeous bread pudding has heady aromas and is served topped with a buttery vanilla sauce made of apple juice, light butter, and a tip of vanilla! Fall is definitely in the air!

Nonstick cooking spray
1 1/2 cups 2% milk
2 eggs
3/4 cup canned pumpkin
1/4 cup plus 1 Tbsp sugar, divided
3 Tbsp light butter with canola oil, divided
1 Tbsp pumpkin pie spice
2 tsp vanilla extract, divided
1/8 tsp salt
8 oz multigrain Italian loaf bread, torn into small pieces
1 1/4 cups water
1 (18-inch-long) sheet aluminum foil
3/4 cup apple juice
1 1/2 tsp cornstarch

1   Coat a 7-inch nonstick springform pan with cooking spray.

2   Whisk together the milk, eggs, pumpkin, 1/4 cup of the sugar, 2 Tbsp of the light butter, the pumpkin pie spice, 1 tsp of the vanilla extract, and salt in a large bowl until well blended. Add the bread cubes and toss to coat well. Let stand for 10 minutes to allow the bread to absorb the milk mixture, stirring occasionally. Place the bread mixture into the springform pan; press down on the bread with the back of a spoon.

3   Place the water and a trivet in the Instant Pot. Cover the springform pan entirely with foil. Make a foil sling by folding an 18-inch-long piece of foil in half lengthwise. Place the pan in the center of the sling and lower the pan into the pot. Fold down the excess foil from the sling to allow the lid to close properly.

4   Seal the lid, close the valve, and set the Manual/Pressure Cook button to 40 minutes.

5 Use a natural pressure release for 10 minutes, followed by a quick pressure release. When the valve drops, carefully remove the lid. Remove the pan and sling carefully using the ends of the foil. Remove the foil from the springform pan. Let stand for 15 minutes to cool.

6 Meanwhile, remove the trivet and discard the water in the pot. Whisk together the apple juice and cornstarch in a small bowl. Press the Cancel button and set to Sauté. Then press the Adjust button to "More" or "High." Add the juice mixture and the remaining 1 Tbsp of sugar to the pot. Bring to a boil and boil for 1 minute, or until thickened, stirring constantly. Remove the insert from the Instant Pot, and stir in the remaining 1 Tbsp of light butter and 1 tsp of vanilla extract.

7 Cut the bread pudding into 8 wedges and serve topped with the sauce.

NUTRITION FACTS

Choices/Exchanges: 1 Starch, 1 Carbohydrate, 1 Lean Protein

Calories: 190; Calories from Fat: 50; Total Fat: 6.0 g; Saturated Fat: 2.0 g; Trans Fat: 0.0 g; Cholesterol: 55 mg; Sodium: 230 mg; Potassium: 230 mg; Total Carbohydrate: 28 g; Dietary Fiber: 3 g; Sugars: 15 g; Protein: 7 g; Phosphorus: 145 mg

Strawberry Wedges with Sweetened Yogurt

SERVES: 8   **SERVING SIZE:** 1/8 cake (1 wedge) plus 1 Tbsp yogurt mixture and 1/4 cup berry mixture
HANDS-ON TIME: 15 minutes   **HANDS-OFF TIME:** 34 minutes   **TOTAL TIME:** 49 minutes (plus 8 hours chill time)

Chia seeds are a close cousin to poppy seeds as far as their texture in baked goods is concerned, but they contain a lot more fiber! You can prepare the base and toppings today, but wait to assemble until the next day for peak flavor and texture. It *does* make a delicious difference!

1 (7-oz) package blueberry muffin mix (such as Jiffy)
1 1/4 cups water, divided
3 Tbsp chia seeds
2 tsp canola oil
2 tsp grated lemon zest
Nonstick cooking spray
1 (18-inch-long) sheet aluminum foil

Toppings:
4 cups strawberries, sliced
1/3 cup water
4 tsp sugar, divided
1/2 cup plain 2% Greek yogurt (such as Fage)
1 tsp vanilla extract

1 Combine the muffin mix, 1/4 cup of the water, the chia seeds, oil, and lemon zest in a medium bowl. Stir until just blended. Spoon into a 7-inch nonstick springform pan coated with cooking spray. Smooth the muffin mixture with the back of a spoon to cover the bottom of the pan evenly.

2 Place 1 cup of the water and a trivet in the Instant Pot. Cover the springform pan entirely with foil.

3 Make a foil sling by folding an 18-inch-long piece of foil in half lengthwise. Place the pan in the center of the sling and lower the pan into the pot. Fold down the excess foil from the sling to allow the lid to close properly. Seal the lid, close the valve, and set the Manual/Pressure Cook button to 30 minutes.

4 Use a quick pressure release. Meanwhile, prepare the toppings. Combine the strawberries, 1/3 cup of water, and 2 tsp of the sugar in a medium bowl. Using a potato masher, lightly mash the strawberries. In a small bowl, combine the yogurt, remaining 2 tsp of sugar, and vanilla extract. Stir until well blended. Separately, cover the yogurt and strawberries with plastic wrap and refrigerate until ready to serve.

5 When the valve drops, carefully remove the lid. Remove the springform pan using the sling. Blot off any excess moisture that is on the foil before removing. Remove the foil and allow to cool completely. Then cover and refrigerate for at least 8 hours or overnight.

6 At time of serving, cut the base into 8 wedges. Spoon 1 Tbsp of the yogurt mixture onto each wedge and top with 1/4 cup of the strawberry mixture and its juices.

NUTRITION FACTS

Choices/Exchanges: 1 Starch, 1/2 Fruit, 1/2 Carbohydrate, 1 Fat

Calories: 190; Calories from Fat: 60; Total Fat: 7.0 g; Saturated Fat: 1.9 g; Trans Fat: 0.0 g; Cholesterol: 5 mg; Sodium: 220 mg; Potassium: 180 mg; Total Carbohydrate: 29 g; Dietary Fiber: 4 g; Sugars: 14 g; Protein: 4 g; Phosphorus: 135 mg

Crunchy Chocolate Chip–Apple Bowl

SERVES: 4   **SERVING SIZE:** 3/4 cup apple mixture and about 3 Tbsp nut mixture
HANDS-ON TIME: 17 minutes   **HANDS-OFF TIME:** 17 minutes   **TOTAL TIME:** 34 minutes

The natural sweetness of the apple is locked in by the pressure-cooking process! And by cooking with a small amount of water, a natural syrup is formed while keeping the apple chunks slightly tender-crisp. The apple mixture is topped with a sweet-and-salty, chocolatey, nutty topping. This recipe brings out the kid in us all!

- 1/3 cup low-fat cereal with granola (such as Special K)
- 1/3 cup unsalted peanuts
- 1 cup plus 2 Tbsp water, divided
- 1 lb apples (such as Gala), halved, cored, and cut into 1-inch chunks
- 1 Tbsp raisins
- 1 tsp ground cinnamon, divided
- 1/4 tsp ground nutmeg
- 1 (18-inch-long) sheet aluminum foil
- 1/4 tsp salt
- 2 1/2 Tbsp mini semi-sweet chocolate chips or 3 Tbsp butterscotch chips, chopped

1. Press the Sauté button, then press the Adjust button to "More" or "High." When the display says "Hot," add the cereal and peanuts to the Instant Pot. Cook for 4 minutes, or until peanuts begin to brown, stirring occasionally. Remove and set aside.

2. Press the Cancel button. Place 1 cup of the water and a trivet in the Instant Pot.

3. Place the apples, raisins, and remaining 2 Tbsp of water in a 7-inch metal or heatproof bowl that will fit in the pot. Sprinkle with 1/2 tsp of the cinnamon and the nutmeg. Cover tightly with foil.

4. Make a foil sling by folding an 18-inch-long piece of foil in half lengthwise. Place the bowl in the center of the sling and lower the bowl into the pot. Fold down the excess foil from the sling to allow the lid to close properly. Seal the lid, close the valve, and set the Manual/Pressure Cook button to 12 minutes.

5   Use a quick pressure release. Meanwhile, place the peanut mixture in a small plastic bag with the remaining 1/2 tsp of cinnamon and the salt. Seal the plastic bag and coarsely crumble the peanut mixture by tapping with a meat mallet or the bottom of a can or bottle.

6   When the valve drops, carefully remove the lid. Remove the bowl using the sling. Blot off any excess moisture that is on the foil before removing. Remove the foil. Spoon equal amounts of the apples and syrup into 4 bowls, top evenly with the nut mixture, and sprinkle with the chocolate chips.

NUTRITION FACTS

Choices/Exchanges: 1/2 Starch, 1 Fruit, 1/2 Carbohydrate, 1 1/2 Fat

Calories: 210; Calories from Fat: 80; Total Fat: 9.0 g; Saturated Fat: 2.5 g; Trans Fat: 0.0 g; Cholesterol: 0 mg; Sodium: 170 mg; Potassium: 260 mg; Total Carbohydrate: 31 g; Dietary Fiber: 5 g; Sugars: 19 g; Protein: 5 g; Phosphorus: 90 mg

Index

Note: Page numbers followed by *ph* refer to photographs